Blending Cultures:
A Journey of Identity in Lakota Country

Tracy Hauff

19th Century Map of Russia and Ukraine

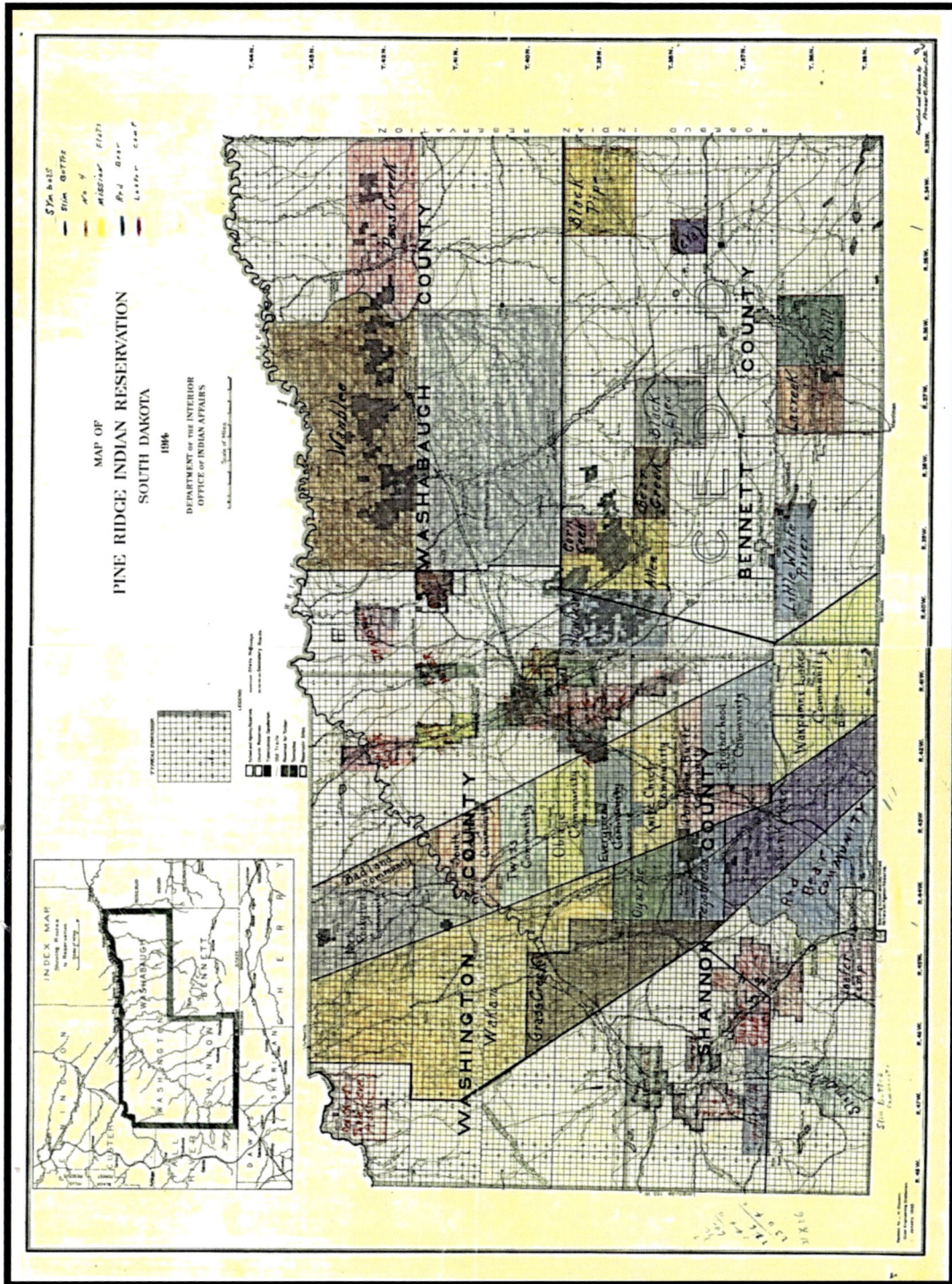

1914 Map of the Pine Ridge Reservation

ISBN: 979-8-3431-8994-0

Cover photo by Kim Lathe
Cover Design by Tracy Hauff

This book is dedicated to the loving memory of my father,

Sylvan Racine Hauff

Gardening was his happy place.

ACKNOWLEDGMENTS

My deepest and most heartfelt gratitude to:

My father, for sharing his profound memories that inspired me to rekindle the Hauff, Brown, and Rooks family saga. I am deeply grateful for the sacrifices you made, which allowed your children to grow up in a better world. Pilamayaye. Tečihila.

April and Mike Gustafson, for your steadfast belief in me and unwavering support of my writing journey. The life of a writer is often isolating and financially uncertain, but you two make sure all is well in my world. Pilamayaye. Tečihila.

The devoted family members who understood the significance of preserving our legacy and took on the invaluable responsibility of safeguarding our family documents and photographs. Pilamayaye.

The historians, whose dedication to research and skill in interpreting the past provided my story with clarity and depth. Your meticulous documentation made it possible to piece together the intricate puzzle of my family history. Pilamayaye.

The librarians and archivists, whose passion and patience are unmatched. Your tireless work in assisting with questions and sourcing rare documents has been a cornerstone of this project. Pilamayaye.

TABLE OF CONTENTS

PREFACE

PART ONE

PART TWO

PART THREE

PREFACE

In 2014, while decluttering my parent's basement, I found two legal pads filled with cursive writing. I recognized the neat penmanship of my father, Sylvan Hauff, and thumbing through the pages, I realized it was a chronicle of his ancestry and early life derived from oral family history and his personal memories. In the first paragraph, he states his wish to share it with future generations. I read his manuscript and put it away.

In 2022, two years after he left us for the spirit world, I felt a sense of urgency to fulfill his wish. After transcribing the intriguing family saga, I was compelled to investigate further, and the result is Part Three of this book. All photos and documents were interspersed by me and were not part of Sylvan's original writing; however, many belong to his collections of photographs and mementos. All the writing in Parts One and Two are Sylvan's narratives as he wrote them. I contributed minimal editing, believing it important to keep his thoughts and words intact.

Sylvan Racine Hauff was an unpretentious, honorable man with a heightened need for intellectual enrichment. His colleagues admired him for his knowledge, calm demeanor, and stellar work ethic during his lifelong career in the criminal justice system. He achieved the highest position in the U.S. Department of Justice Federal Probation Program when he was promoted to Chief Federal Probation Officer for the state of South Dakota. As a devoted husband, father, and grandfather who put his family first above all else, he was loved by his wife, Margaret, and seven children—April, Steven, Tracy, Echo, Alison, Brad, and Brian—his grandchildren and great-grandchildren.

Born into poverty on the Rosebud Indian Reservation during the Great Depression, he took considerable pride in homeownership and was the most resourceful man I have ever met, skilled at home repair and Do-It-Yourself projects long before the existence of YouTube and HGTV. He restored old furniture, toys, tricycles, and bicycles and grew lush vegetable gardens and fragrant beds of flowers. Our house displayed fresh bouquets of gladiolas, roses, tulips, carnations, and snapdragons during the summer. Dad was my encyclopedia, a father who always had time to impart essential or trivial wisdom and delighted in doing so. His dry, keen sense of humor was delivered with such a deadpan expression that it took me several childhood years to understand he was joking and not serious. His wit generated numerous eye rolls from his children when they reached their teenage years.

In addition to his familial duties, he was a leader at his office, a problem solver and counselor for his probationers and parolees, a mentor for attorneys fresh out of law school, a decade-long appointed member of The South Dakota Indian Affairs Commission, an instructor of college-level police science courses, a trainer in law enforcement, a prolific reader and orator of Native Studies, a county fair blue-ribbon vintner, and a spellbinding storyteller.

Most people wish to leave their mark on the world before passing into the afterlife, and Sylvan did just that. He profoundly and positively affected many lives, focusing on the marginalized villages on the South Dakota Indian reservations. I have met numerous people in South Dakota from all levels of society who asked me if Sylvan was my father. When I would affirm this, their first remark was always in the context of "He is/was a really great guy," and they would then recall a poignant anecdote regarding their connection with him.

One such story came from my friend, Alex White Plume. His encounter with Sylvan was similar to others. As a young man, Alex found himself in a confusing situation on the wrong side of the law. Raised on the Pine Ridge reservation in a household that spoke only Lakota, Alex did not understand the circumstances of his arrest. He was taken to Pennington County Jail, where no one could communicate with him. Sylvan learned of Alex's predicament and went to see him. "Oh, I was never so happy to see anyone in my life," Alex recalled. "He started speaking Lakota and told me he was there to help me. I knew then it was going to be okay." Sylvan arranged for Alex's release on bail, placing him temporarily with a family in Rapid City until his court date. "After court, he drove me home to Manderson and made visits until I was off probation. He had a good sense of humor, like mine," Alex chuckled. "I was serious about my situation, but we laughed together, too."

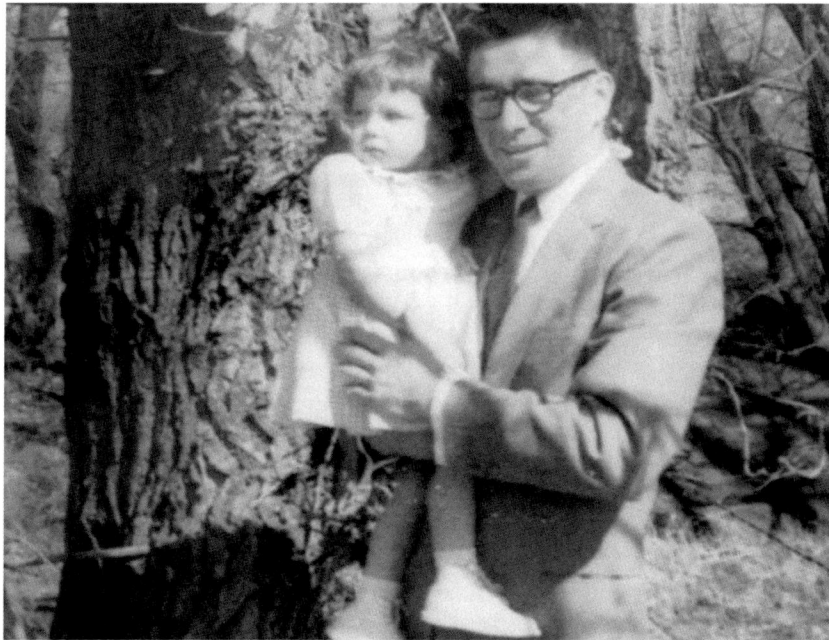

Sylvan and Tracy Hauff, 1956

PART ONE

The Immigration of Johannes and Maria Hauf

German-Russians on the Reservation

Rapid City Indian Boarding School

Manuscript by Sylvan Hauff

Compiled and edited by Tracy Hauff

THE IMMIGRATION OF JOHANNES AND MARIA HAUF

Having recently observed my sixty-fifth birthday and been awakened to a need to communicate with the future, I have decided to try to record some of the salient features and occurrences of my life and a little of my personal history and that of my antecedents in the unlikely event that one of my descendants might someday have a passing curiosity concerning some aspect of these admittedly rather mundane matters.

I will first present my observations and recollections of my parents and their individual backgrounds and the course of their lives. My father, William August Hauff, was born at home on his parent's homestead in Boyd County, near Naper, Nebraska, on August 3, 1900. He was the sixth of nine children born to Johannes Hauff and Maria Elizabeth Lenaschmidt, who emigrated from the Czarist empire of Russia and came to the United States in 1888. Johannes, my paternal grandfather, was born and raised in Ukraine, north of the Black Sea, part of Odesa, and was the youngest son of successful farmer/ranchers Johann Georg and Marie Hauf. Both Johannes and Maria were descendants of ethnic Germans whose ancestors had immigrated to Imperial Russia sometime during or after the reign of Catherine the Great, the German princess who became Empress of Russia in 1700 and at whose personal invitation thousands of German peasants and business entrepreneurs left their ancestral homeland and settled in the sparsely populated and primitive regions of southern and eastern Russia. The thrifty, hardworking Russians from Germany turned these regions into the breadbasket of Russia, just as Catherine knew they would, but staunchly retained their native language and culture and lived in exclusively German settlements.

Maria, an orphan who lived with an older brother, was born and raised in the Volga River province of Saratov in a colony known as Huck, many miles east of Odessa. It is not known how Maria happened to marry Johannes Hauf, but it is considered likely that theirs was an arranged marriage, as was the common practice in that time and place, and that the young couple probably knew each other prior to their marriage. The circumstances of Maria's orphanhood are not known. Johannes was eighteen years old, and Maria was sixteen when they set out on the journey to transplant the Hauf clan to the new world.

It is not known how many generations of the Hauf and Lenaschmidt families lived in Russia following their emigration from Germany, when these emigrations occurred, or exactly where in Germany the families had their origins. Various histories record a pattern of the emigrations, which usually involved entire families, kinship groups, villages, or religious congregations making the journey and transition together and settling together in the same regions of Russia. Apparently, there was no organized governmental resistance to this departure on the part of German authorities. There was usually a community transplantation that took place, with most preexisting kinship ties and relationships continuing with only a change in geography. The German immigrants were overwhelmingly farmers and peasants. Once landed in Russia, the groups quickly established a new community, which closely resembled the one they left behind in Germany, often retaining the same name as the village left behind. The German settlements in Russia were essentially colonies, each of which was relatively self-sufficient and self-governing.

The imperial Russian government furnished transportation for the immigrants, naturalized them as citizens when they crossed into the Czar's domain, gave them tracts of land, and provided grants and loans to become established as farmers and small businessmen. The native Russians in those regions were basically serfs, illiterate and socially backward, and unable to exploit the richness of their agrarian environment. Catherine hoped that her immigrant German kinsmen would inoculate the native Russians with their inherent skills, ambition, thriftiness, and resourcefulness. However, the German enclaves remained largely closed social units, and the local populace was relatively uncontaminated by the foreign presence. The Germans in Russia were good citizens of the new land, paying their taxes, maintaining good social order, and contributing substantially to the economic growth and improvement of their adoptive homeland, but interaction with Indigenous Russians was rather limited, and intermarriage was infrequent.

Students of European history can attest to the frequent, devastating, and bloody wars that repeatedly swept over the countries of central Europe and decimated their populations from the time of the Roman Empire and to the fact that much of Germany lay in the path of one or another of numerous different invading armies, as the brutal monarchs battled each other over land, power, and religion. No sooner had the peasantry recovered from one such destructive invasion, which left its populace in utter ruin and starvation, than another war would commence, to be fought largely in their homeland. In taking up Catherine's offer of free land and security, and freedom from military conscription for at least 100 years, the Germans must have thought they had been killed in another invasion of their homeland and gone to heaven! Moreover, the lands to which they traveled and to which they were given clear titles were unusually rich and productive, unlike the played-out soils of their original homeland, which had been tilled intensively for hundreds of years. The armies of imperial Rome had never grazed their horses on the virgin grasses of the Russian Steppes, where rich black soil lay five feet deep in many places.

Powerful, resolute, and benevolent toward her subjects as Catherine was, she was not immortal. With her passing, the monarchy reverted to a succession of less sympathetic Czars, who were unwilling to continue Catherine's pledge to the German-Russian subjects now settled in Ukraine and the Volga River regions, particularly with respect to their exemption from mandatory military service. Napoleon Bonaparte had cost many Russian lives in his massive invasion, and the Czar had other wars to fight and needed every available soldier he could find among his subjects. Native Russians resented the special exemption enjoyed by their German-speaking countrymen, and it became increasingly difficult to honor Catherine's pledge. Eventually, the exemption from the draft was abrogated, and the young male descendants of the original German immigrants found themselves wearing the uniform of Imperial Russia.

The departure of Johannes and Maria from Russia to America was a precipitous one. The imperial government of Russia had long since abrogated the agreement between Czarina Catherine and her loyal German-Russian subjects, which guaranteed that they would not be conscripted for military duty, and all Johannes' older brothers had been drafted and had served the mandatory period of six years in the Czar's army. At age 18, Johannes was on the verge of being inducted when he and Maria left their village in the middle of the night and made their way to the Austrian border. Russia needed every available conscript, and to attempt to leave the country under these circumstances was to risk death or long imprisonment if apprehended. Johannes and Maria were assisted by Jewish villagers on their flight to the border and were obliged to swim a river that formed the border between Russia and Austria. When they emerged from the water, they were confronted by Austrian border guards, who were inclined to turn them over to Russian counterparts, but when the young couple addressed the guards in German and persuaded them that they were citizens of Austria out for a nightly swim, they were permitted to leave and make their way inland.

They eventually proceeded to the Atlantic coast and got passage on a liner for New York. By railroad, they traveled to Sioux City, Iowa, and then overland to Olivet, in Hutchinson County, in the brand-new state of South Dakota, which was admitted to the Union in 1889. Several of their relatives from Russia, who had immigrated earlier, had taken up homesteads in Hutchinson County, and Johannes and Maria had their help in getting established in this new and entirely strange land.

Although Johannes spoke and could read and write in German and Russian, neither he nor Maria knew a word of English. It can be reasonably inferred that their families had been among the earlier emigrants to Russia, and that the families had lived in Russia for enough generations to have lost all ties with their original homeland and all knowledge of its precise location.

Parents of Johannes Hauf.
Johann Georg Hauf, born in 1820, in Merkel, Volga Region, Russia. Died in 1890 in South Dakota.
Marie Elizabeth Specht Hauf, born in 1822, in Merkel, Volga Region, Russia. Died in 1908 in South Dakota.

Johannes Hauff, son of Johann Georg and Maria, was born May 6, 1869, in Y.E. Radrinader, Russia. He immigrated to the United States in 1888. He died April 7, 1942, in Rapid City, South Dakota.
Marie Elizabeth Leneschmidt Hauff was born December 17, 1870, in Saratov, Russia. She immigrated to the United States in 1888 with Johannes. She died September 29, 1963, in Rapid City, South Dakota.
(Photo courtesy of Jack and Shirley McGuire's Book, Hauf Germany 2001)

Johannes is photographed in America wearing his Russian papakha and long winter overcoat.

When portions of northcentral Nebraska were opened for homesteading, Johannes and Maria moved there and took out homestead land near the town of Naper, where they built a sod house and began farming the land.

To supplement their income, Johannes, who had a distinct flair for languages and who learned English in a very short time, qualified as a rural mail carrier and worked at this job for a time. A number of his relatives had also homesteaded in the same area, and at times, there was confusion in getting the mail to the right parties, as some had the same given Christian names, as did Johannes and a cousin. To remedy his situation, Johannes was persuaded to add a final f to his surname, which then became Hauff. This was already an ancient and well-known name in Germany, immortalized by the famous literary figure Wilhelm Hauff and by that prominent and highly respected brewery, the Hauff Braurei, one of the largest in Germany, established in 1491. One of my most prized possessions is a set of pilsner glasses with the Hauff imprimatur, sent from Germany by my niece, Kathleen, whose husband was stationed there with the army in 1992.

Not long after Johannes and Maria arrived in the United States, Johannes' parents disposed of their considerable land holdings, livestock, and other property in Ukraine and emigrated to this country to join their children, all of whom had been assisted by the parents in moving here a few years earlier. The older Hauffs lived near Tripp, South Dakota.

Johannes and Maria embraced their new homeland wholeheartedly, eventually Americanizing their given names to reflect their status and insisted on being called John and

Mary. They were farmers, as were countless generations of their antecedents in both Germany and Russia, and they prospered in the new land. They were among the true pioneers in the midwestern United States, whose most precious assets were their Christian religious faith and their inborn German culture, which emphasized hard work, clean living, thriftiness, cleanliness, and honesty. Arriving as they did, mainly by family groups, and settling in large, closely linked rural neighborhoods which resembled the German colonies they had occupied in Russia, they continued to retain the language and most of the cultural trappings of their ancient heritage while absorbing as much as they could of what the new world had to offer them. Mostly, they created their own world in what was essentially a wilderness area, but the new country welcomed them with open arms and allowed them freedom as most of them had never known in the old country, and they rejoiced in their extreme good fortune.

In her native Saratov, Mary had acquired a lot of knowledge of effective folk remedies for various ailments and disorders and learned midwifery and other medical skills. In an age and place where physicians and nurses were virtually unknown on the wild prairies of Nebraska and South Dakota, she soon gained a reputation in her community as a healer and applied her knowledge and skills among her neighbors on the frontier, often being away from home for several days while attending a sick or injured homesteader or delivering a new baby. She also delivered nine healthy children of her own, all at home and without professional medical assistance. She raised and preserved large quantities of food, designed and sewed all her family's clothing, and saw to it that each of her children acquired a solid foundation in evangelical Lutheran religion and were confirmed in this exacting and conservative faith. When Smallpox swept through the region and afflicted many of the homesteaders, the Hauff family was protected from the scourge. Mary obtained cowpox exudate from an afflicted neighbor girl and carefully vaccinated each of them, using the same method later adopted by most physicians, making several small scratches on the arm and rubbing the exudate into them.

Although his farming operations were reasonably profitable, John Hauff was never keenly attuned to agrarian life. As a boy in Russia and the youngest son of relatively well-to-do parents, he had been allowed to spend much time in study and enjoyed a more leisurely and less toilsome existence than that demanded of a frontier homesteader. After farming his claim in Nebraska, he sold it and purchased property in nearby Gregory County, South Dakota, a few miles south of the present town of Dallas near the early settlement of Carlock. There, he opened a general merchandise store, which he operated for several years while continuing to engage in farming and ranching. Actually, his older children did most of the latter work, while John devoted himself to merchandising. He lost one of his thumbs when it was accidentally amputated by the rim of a large wooden vinegar barrel he was unloading from a wagon. Merchandising was not without its hazards and uncertainties. After several years, the store was destroyed by fire, and John decided to relocate once again.

The first American generation of the Hauff Family. c. 1913.
Back Row: Jake, Fred, John, Carl, Anna
Front Row: Ed, Walter, Johannes (John), Ida, Maria (Mary), William

John and Mary purchased some land a short distance northwest of the Indian village of Okreek, South Dakota, in Todd County in about 1912. They built a home there and raised cattle and were reasonably successful at this.

In 1916, they were doing well enough to make a sightseeing trip to Texas. This proved to be an extended visit and partial relocation, and they spent a year in Texas. They left their two sons, William and Edwin, at home to look after the ranch and care for the livestock, and they traveled to Odessa, Texas. Always an impulsive and ambitious man, John decided to continue for a time at Odessa and purchased a large rooming/boarding house there, which he arranged for Mary to operate. They had made the trip to Texas so that Mary could enjoy a brief holiday and respite from her long and tedious labors, but she was saddled with even more work and responsibility than she had at home. None of her children were very happy about this unexpected and unsettling development.

Back at Okreek, William and Edwin held their own at the ranch, but after a year without their parents and having to fend for themselves and with no immediate prospects of relief, they notified their parents that they were leaving. World War One had just erupted, and William enlisted in the U.S. Army and went to Europe with the American Expeditionary Force, being assigned as a medical corpsman in the 1st Infantry Division.

The elder Hauffs were compelled to abandon their plans, sell their business in Texas, and return to Okreek. I don't believe my grandfather ever completely forgave his sons for their impetuous desertion, even though other family members thought it entirely reasonable, given the circumstances involved and the totally unreasonable expectations of the father.

Private William A. Hauff, WWI, Medical Corps, age 17. 1st Division, 3rd Army of Occupation, Germany.

Photo by United States Army

John Hauff was a product of his old-world upbringing and was inclined to adhere to these outdated and occasionally cruel (by present standards) practices to the detriment of his children and his wife. One such practice involved hiring out his sons to work for neighboring farmers while he collected the son's wages and kept them for himself. When his elder son, Frederick, thus indentured to a farmer, was without warm clothing, boots, gloves, etc., to use in outside work, the employer took it upon himself to purchase these needed items for the boy and to withhold the cost from the boy's wages. When John appeared at the end of the month to collect the wages, he refused to allow the employer to withhold the cost of the clothing, demanded the full months' pay, and lectured the employer to the effect that he, as the boy's father, was responsible for furnishing all of his clothing and that if the boy needed additional clothing, he should have come to him and asked for it. (Presumably, in that event, John would have provided outgrown clothes from an older son, or perhaps his wife sewed the items needed for him). In the end, John prevailed but made few friends for such a rigid and harsh approach to life, even though it had been the accepted way in the old country for countless generations.

My father, William August Hauff, was a remarkably bright, articulate, and resourceful boy who managed to make his presence known even though he was lodged in the middle of eight rather large and aloof siblings. His early schooling was limited to six sparse years when he was not needed to work on the family farm. There were no organized school districts at that time, and William attended a Lutheran church school, held in a sod shanty, where all instruction was in the German language and strongly tinged with Church philosophy and protestant religion. German was spoken exclusively in the Hauff household at that time, although the parents and children also learned English through contact outside the home. William had to learn to read and write English on his own, and he did remarkably well at this. In time, he lost virtually all traces of his German accent, but his parents always retained theirs, as did his older sister, Anna, who married a German-speaking spouse and continued to use her native tongue in her home. William's mother never learned to read or write in English and always wrote in the old German script, which was beautiful in appearance but formidable to decipher.

William was of average height, 5 feet 9 inches, and seldom over 150 pounds in weight. He had gray eyes, straight brown hair, and a medium ruddy complexion. His speech reflected his thought patterns: a rapid outpouring of words that were occasionally difficult to follow due to their rapidity. William was an impatient man, full of nervous energy, but was also a generally tolerant person who always maintained the highest standard of personal decorum, except for his language, which often ran to the profane. William had an excellent sense of humor, a ready smile, and a hearty laugh and was well-liked by most people. Until the final years of his life, he maintained a high level of physical conditioning and activity. A man of many diverse talents, he was an excellent carpenter and mechanic and a good hand with livestock and farm machinery. He was careful and conservative with money and always remained financially sound, even throughout the severe economic depression of the 1930s when thousands of people went bankrupt. He was fiercely independent and thoroughly honest in his dealings with others and had no difficulty borrowing money when needed, which was rare. Living within his income was one of his strongest personal traits.

My dad always dressed well and kept himself well-groomed, and his posture was remarkably erect throughout his lifetime. He loved fishing and hunting with his children, with whom he always displayed great personal interest and concern. It was mainly through his good counsel, encouragement, and financial assistance that each of his children was able to complete college and become established in a sound career field.

Following his return from Europe at the end of World War I, William continued in the Army for a time and was eventually commissioned a Second Lieutenant of Cavalry. But the war to end all wars had been fought, and the interest in national defense waned to the point where a military career seemed pointless, and William requested and was granted a discharge.

Returning to South Dakota, William lived for a time with his parents, who by then had purchased a farm a short distance north of Mission, and again worked as a farm hand. During this period, about 1922, he met and began a romantic relationship with Leona Mattie Brown, a nineteen-year-old Lakota girl who was working as a matron at the Rosebud Indian Boarding School, a federal government facility near Mission.

Wishing to get married and establish his own home and family, William needed a financial stake and some property, which his parents were unable to provide. William left Mission and went to Lead, South Dakota, in the Black Hills to work as an underground miner with the Homestake Mining Company. He saved his wages and lived frugally, and eventually had enough money to get started in a limited way in farming and ranching. On September 12, 1923, he and Leona were married in Lead, South Dakota.

Newlyweds, Mr. and Mrs. William Hauff. September 12, 1923.

Shortly thereafter, William quit Homestake and moved with his wife to a rented farm known as the Clark place, southwest of Parmelee, South Dakota, on the Rosebud Indian Reservation. With only a little equipment and capital but with high hopes and a lot of ambition, he began farming the leased property. At the same time, to supplement his income, he began a partnership with a man named Shorty Reifel, with whom he purchased a truck and started hauling freight from the nearest railroad station at Crookston, Nebraska, to Rosebud Agency and other points in Todd County. Shorty Reifel's eldest son, Ben, who earned a PhD from Harvard University, would much later be elected a United States Congressman for South Dakota.

William and Leona had their first child, William [Billie] Callie Hauff, at home while living on the Clark Place, delivered by William's mother on October 26, 1925. About two years later, they had another son, Vernon Dale Hauff, who lived only two weeks before succumbing to pneumonia, which claimed the lives of many children in those days. Vernon Dale was buried in the Lutheran Cemetery at Mission.

In 1927, William and Leona received a quarter section of Indian Allotment land, raw prairie located about eleven miles northwest of Norris, South Dakota, in Washabaugh County, and moved there with their household goods and livestock. They stayed temporarily with Leona's aunt and uncle, Nancy and Louis Peck, who lived over a high ridge about two miles north, while William constructed a small two-room frame house on their land. William also built some outbuildings and drilled a water well using a hand-operated post-hole digger. He must have experienced great satisfaction when he was finally able to move his wife and son into their very own home, built with his own hands. In time, the Hauffs leased adjacent Indian-owned land and expanded their ranching operations.

In the winter of 1928, Leona gave birth to a son, Richard [Dick] Joseph Hauff, her third child. William took Leona to the government hospital in Rosebud, about 45 miles away, for the delivery on January 13, 1928. As a Lakota woman, Leona was eligible for free medical care provided by the United States Bureau of Indian Affairs (BIA), which was a major consideration in Richard being born in the hospital rather than at home on the prairie without obstetrical assistance. Even so, there were no roads in the vicinity of the Hauff ranch and traveling 45 miles in the wintertime in a less than reliable and unheated vehicle presented its own hazards.

William and Leona were to repeat this trek on November 28, 1929, when my turn came to be born. On that occasion, they arrived barely in time to begin the delivery, and it was necessary for William to physically carry his wife up the steep stairs to the second floor of the hospital, where the delivery room was located.

The late 1920s and 1930s were tough times for nearly everyone in the United States, and dry-land farmers and ranchers in the western states were not spared the economic distress during the Great Depression. In these very unfortunate circumstances, William and Leona staked their claim to their share of the good life and the American dream that had attracted William's parents to this country barely 40 years earlier. For the next 12 years, they struggled to make a living for themselves but managed to survive on the ranch. While they were able to raise small crops of wheat, oats, and barley, as well as a few cattle and horses, there was virtually no market for their produce much of the time.

Living on the ranch and being somewhat more self-sufficient than many less fortunate people, they survived the Dust Bowl days and the great clouds of grasshoppers that devoured their hay and grain before it could be harvested. While the summers were extremely hot and dry, the winters were unusually cold, and the snow piled deep and drifted into small mountains across the plains and over our pastures. My father was often nearly frozen stiff as he rode his fence lines on horseback to keep the cattle from straying, chopped holes in the frozen water for the animals to drink, and cut firewood to heat our house. Winter always enhanced the extreme isolation of our existence, confining us to the two tiny rooms of our home, which measured about 12 feet by 24 feet. There was no electricity or plumbing, no telephone or mail service, and no radio until about 1939. Our only lighting at night was from the kerosene lamps, each of which produced little more illumination than that given by an ordinary candle. Every drop of water used in the home had to be pumped by hand and carried in buckets from the well about 75 yards away. A particularly enervating experience was using the outdoor privy when it was 20 degrees below zero!

My mother cooked all our meals, baked all our bread, and heated our water for bathing and washing clothes on a small 2-burner kerosene stove in the front room of our house, which served as kitchen, dining room, and living room. The other room, with a cloth curtain hanging in the doorway, was our bedroom which held two double beds and my mother's steamer trunk with camelback lid. Our kitchen table had been built by my maternal grandfather, George Racine Brown, out of heavy native cedar wood and was our only real item of household furniture besides the beds and a couple of chairs. We children stood or sat on upturned orange crates for meals.

As a small boy, I recall that it was occasionally necessary to share my meager play area in the front room of the house with a newborn calf brought into the house to keep warm and save it from freezing to death outside. A small pen would be constructed using my mother's large trunk and my father's footlocker. I recall being fascinated by the small animals, but their odor and mess hastened their departure after a few days when they had gained strength, or the weather had improved. The floor then had to be thoroughly scrubbed by my hardworking and fastidious mother before we were permitted to use it for play again. Such experiences were nothing new for the families of early cattle ranchers and farmers and were taken in stride when they occurred.

Few travelers ever ventured far enough off the distant roads to come near the Hauff place, and the times when a lone cowboy would ride in looking for strays were occasions of great excitement for the children. I can still hear the sound of the spurs on their boots as they walked up the path to our door. Most of these men were friendly enough but unmarried and childless themselves and disinclined to talk very much. Many were Lakota relatives of my mother. My mother always gave them coffee and perhaps a left-over cinnamon bun if there were any. They stayed a little while and passed on any news they might have to share, and my father always seemed to enjoy their visits. Sometimes, I would water their horses at the windmill my father eventually erected. I had to be careful while examining their saddles and bridles as the horses were sometimes spooky broncs who were not accustomed to being handled by children.

In the spring of 1932, on June 10th, my sister, Luella Ilene Hauff, was born in our house, with my grandmother, Mary Hauff, in attendance. Although I was only 2 ½ years old, I have a vague recollection of this event, particularly of hearing the baby crying in the house immediately after birth. My two brothers and I had been ushered outside by my grandmother and instructed to remain outside for a time, but I do not recall having any advance warning or explanation as to what was taking place. Luella's arrival abruptly ended my own favored status as the youngest child, and since she was a girl, she easily claimed the lion's share of attention thereafter. With no other children living anywhere near, the Hauff children were obliged to play together and look out for one another, and we three older brothers were particularly fond of our baby sister, who was a pretty child with auburn hair and brown eyes.

The nearest town was Norris, a tiny Indian village eleven miles away, where there were two stores, a gasoline station, a beer tavern, and the Black Pipe State Bank, which was owned by my father's closest friend and advisor, O.A. Hodson. Dad always stopped and visited with "Hod" when he went to town, which was about every other week when the weather was favorable. At that time, he would sell his accumulation of cream at the cream station, pick up his mail at the post office and buy the groceries at the Greenwood store.

Sometimes I would accompany my parents to Norris, and I was always fascinated by the sights, sounds, and smells of this place. The village was composed of small cabins occupied by Indian families. I recall being particularly interested in the large bunch of bananas that was suspended from a ceiling joist in the store and the large roll of wrapping paper and cotton cord used to wrap meat in the store. In those days, five dollars would buy a large box of assorted groceries, and the grocer never failed to include a small sack of mixed candies for the children without charge. At home, these treats were kept on a high shelf, carefully rationed out to the children, and made to last at least two full weeks. I have no recollection of ever having bottled soda pop or candy bars, but in summer, my father would sometimes spring for a 5-cent ice cream cone, which I found almost indescribably delicious. Surprisingly, a long metal can that contained the ice cream, encased in a thick insulated canvas bag, would preserve the ice cream in a frozen state for a month or more, and there was no mechanical refrigeration in use in the store or anywhere in these pre-RCA times.

I distinctly remember my first encounter with a concrete sidewalk. The ground at Norris was quite sandy, and when my mother walked across the sidewalk in front of the Black Pipe

Bank, the soles of her shoes made a loud crackly sound that caught my attention. I had never seen a sidewalk of any kind before or even heard anyone walk on one.

Franklin Roosevelt's New Deal ushered in a number of economic relief programs intended to benefit those farmers and ranchers who had not lost their land through mortgage foreclosure and were still hanging on by their teeth. My father obtained a $200 government feed and seed loan and managed to plant his crops another year. Virtually everyone was dirt poor and hard-pressed to put food on their tables; the only consolation was that we were all in the same boat. I do not ever recall realizing or feeling that we were poor; in fact, since we were able to produce most of our own food and fuel, we were probably a little better off than many of our neighbors, who were obliged to stand in line for food relief in such places as Wanblee, SD about 20 miles west of our place. When emergency employment programs, such as Works Progress Administration (WPA) and Public Works Administration (PWA), were initiated, my father signed up to build roads and stock dams and spent quite a bit of time away from home working with his team of horses, Jim and Cricket.

My mother, Leona Mattie Brown, was born at Cut Meat Creek, near the present town of Parmelee, South Dakota, on the Rosebud Indian Reservation on November 22, 1903, the sixth of nine children of George Racine Brown and Susie Rooks. Her father, who was one-quarter Sioux Indian, had been born and raised in northeastern Colorado, where his father, Joseph Brown, Sr., a former Union cavalryman from Ohio, was engaged in freighting. George R. Brown had been among those Indian children recruited to attend distant boarding schools operated by the federal government and had spent six years at the Carlisle Institute in Pennsylvania.

After leaving Carlisle, he joined the Wild West Show, owned and managed by Buffalo Bill Cody, and spent a couple of years traveling with the show as a trick rider and roper. George was a handsome and talented man and a born showman with a great fondness for horses, parades, rodeos, and the like.

Center: William "Buffalo Bill" Cody
Far right: George R. Brown

My maternal grandmother, Susie Rooks Brown, was one-half Oglala Sioux and the daughter of Joseph Rooks, Sr., and his full-blood Oglala wife, Tiŋgleška (Fawn). Joseph Rooks was a former Union cavalryman from Missouri who settled in northeastern Colorado following his discharge after the Civil War. In his affidavit of 1910, he states he married Tiŋgleška according to the Lakota custom by trading her family a horse for her hand in marriage.

By some accounts, Joseph and Tiŋgleška Rooks were present and in attendance at the Black Hills Treaty Conference of 1868 at Ft. Laramie, Wyoming Territory. It is believed that my grandmother, Susie, was born at Ft. Laramie in the summer of 1868, although some accounts have her birthplace as Ft. Randall, Dakota Territory, on the Missouri River, some 350 miles northeast of Ft. Laramie, as the crow flies. Joseph and Tiŋgleška had two other children, Joseph Jr., and Frank, before Tiŋgleška died while they were living in the vicinity of Ft. Robinson in present-day Dawes County, Nebraska.

My maternal great-grandfather, Joseph Rooks, Sr., then married Katheryn (Kate) Robinson, a mixed-blood Lakota woman, and fathered fifteen additional children by her. With the establishment of the Pine Ridge Indian Reservation, he gained employment with the U.S. Indian Field Service as a District Administrator or Boss Farmer and worked in that capacity for many years at Manderson and Allen, South Dakota. He and his family were at Manderson when the tragic incident between the Miniconjou band of Chief Big Foot and elements of the 7th Cavalry Regiment occurred at Wounded Knee, about 8 miles away, in December of 1890.

Not much is known about the life of my grandmother, Susie Rooks, prior to her marriage to George R. Brown. Certainly, she was fluent in both English and Lakota and was a woman of exemplary character and good upbringing, for she imparted many of these positive attributes to her children. Whether she ever attended school or to what extent she could read or write is unknown. She was held in high esteem and respected by all members of her family and was a devoted wife and loving mother. She died while I was an infant.

After leaving the Wild West Show, getting married, and starting a family, my maternal grandfather, George R. Brown, opened a trading post at Cut Meat Creek on the Rosebud Reservation and made his living as a licensed Indian Trader. My mother and several of the other children were born at Cut Meat during this period.

the list of goods for the most amount
of money

GEO. R. BROWN,

Clearing Sale   INDIAN TRADER,   *you get the goods*
for the same
CUT MEAT DISTRICT.   *price they cost me*
ROSEBUD AGENCY,
S. DAKOTA.

$2.00 blankets for $1.00
$6.00 wool " " 4.00

1906.

Price List for the Month of *March* —189—

Allspice, Taspan opemnipi icahiye	60 to 40	Lamp Chimneys, Petijanjan janjan.	25 to 15
Axle grease, Campagmiyan islaye	to 40	Ladies' hose, Winyau tohunyakon,.	to
Axes, Mazunspe. *Complete 148*	to 100	Matches, Yuwilepi.	to
Bacon, Kukuse sin.	16 to 15	Milk, condensed, Asanpi mas wognaka.	to
Baking powder, Winakapo	to	Mustard, btl., Wicahiyutapizi.	to
Brooms, Owangicahinte.	52 to 30	Macaroni, Wahanpi icahiye.	to
Butcher knives, Mina ikceka.	75 to 50	Muslin, bleached, Mnihuha ska zizipela	to
Burners, lamp, Petijanjan el maza ostanpi	5 to 24	Muslin, unbleached, Mnihuha ska soka.	10 to 7
Boots, Canhanpa iskahuhanska.	5 to 3	Men's hose, Wica tahunyakon	to 6
Buttons, pearl, Ceskikan kogli	to 5	Mosquito nets, capongwokeya.	to
Buttons, china, Ceskikan ska.	to 24	Nails, Maswiyokatan.	6 to 4
Buttons, rubber, Ceskikan sapa	to	Nutmegs, Wastemna wicahi waspan yanpi	to
Beads, seed, Psito iwaksu	15 to 10	Neckties, Tahuska inapin	50 to 25
Beads, brass, Psito, maza	to	Oatmeal, Wayahota yukpanpi.	20 to 10
Beads, necklace, Psito wanapin	to	Oil, coal, Petijanjan wigli	35 to 30
Bobs. ear. Swula.	72 to 5	Oil cans, Petijanjan wigli iyokastan	60 to 40
Bowls, tin, Maza wiyatke	to	Overalls, Akaul onzoge.	100 to 75
Coffee, green, Pejutasapa spansni.	to 15	Pepper, black, Yamnumugapi.	10 to 8
Coffee, roasted, Pejutasapa spau	to 15	Pickles, Wicohiyutapi toto.	to
Crackers. Aguyapi saka	15 to 12	Pants, Onzoge.	to
Can goods, Maswoguake.	to 30	Pans, dish, Waksica tanka.	80 to 50
Candies, Canhanpi hanska.	to	Plates, tin, Maswaksica.	10 to 05
Candies, Petijanjan ska.	20 to 15	Pocket knives, Mina yuksijapi.	to 50
Cigarettes. Mnihuha cannupa kogapi	to	Pocket books, Mazaska ojaha.	to 30
Cheese, Asanpi igli suta.	25 to 15	Rice, Psin.	to 5
Chocolate. Canha yukpanpi kalyapi.	to	Raisins, Canwiyapehe.	15 to 10
Coffee pots, Wikalye	to 50	Ropes, Hahionta wikon	70 to 15
Cloves, Hi iyatinze.	to	Sugar, Canhanpi ska	to
Calicoes, Mnihuha ikceka	10 to 05	Salt, Miniskuya.	to
Cigarette paper, Mnihuha cannupa	to	Soap, laundry, Haipajaja onwojajapi	to 5
Canton flannel, Mnihuha okischinsma	15 to 10	Soap, toilet, Haipajaja iglujajapi	to 5
Cloth, blue. Sinato	to 185	Soda, Winakapo zi	to
Children's hose, Wakanheja tohunyakon	to 20	Starch, corn, Wipatinye sponyanpi	10 to 7
Combs, Nasunpakca.	to	Starch, gloss, Ogle ipatinye.	10 to 6
Drawers, men's, Mahel unzoge.	75 to 40	Sardines, Hogan maswognaka blaska.	25 to 15
Dried fruit. Taspa puza	15 to 12	Syrup, Tuhimaga canhanpi.	80 to 20
Flour. Aguyapi blu.	to	Shears, Iynsila	25 to 15
Fish lines and hooks. Hoicuwa na maza.	to	Shawls, Sinahaswupi	to
Ginghams. Mnihuha can iyapehanpi	to 10	Suits, men's, Wica hayapi	to 5
Goggles, Istamaza ogetonpi	to	Suits, boys', Hoksila hayapi	to 250
Hair, pipes, Wawoslata.	to 6	Shoes, men's, Wica tacanhanpa.	to
Handkerchief, silk, Wapahilate itipakinte	to 10	Shoes, ladies', Winyan tacanhanpa.	to
Handkerchief, cotton, Itipokinte ikceka	to 10	Shoes, boys', Hoksila tacanhanpa.	to
Ham, Kukuse ceca ojutonpi.	to	Shoes, children's, Hoksicala tacanhanpa	75
Hats, men's, Wapostan wica tawa	to	Tea, Wahipa kalyapi	to
Hats, boys', Wapostan Hoksila tawa	to	Tobacco, smoking, Canli yukpanpi	to
Hoods, baby's, Hoksicala tawapostan	to	Tobacco, chewing, Canli ikceka.	to
Jumbles, Aguyapi skuya cokaya ohiloka	to 15	Table knives and forks, Mina na wicape.	to
Knobs, door, and lock, Tiyopa inatoke	to	Thread, cotton, Hahionta wicagege ikceka.	to
Lye, Cahiota hanpi wispanye.	to	Thread, silk, Hahionta wicagege wapahilate	to
Laundry blue, Itoye.	to	Towels, Iteipakinte.	25 to 15
Lard, Wigli	15 to 14	Wash tubs, Kokawoyujaja.	to
Lamps, Petijanjan	to	Wash boards, Wipaskiskite.	to

Everything go at cost except groceries

GEORGE R. BROWN, INDIAN TRADER

CUT MEAT DISTRICT   ROSEBUD AGENCY, S. DAKOTA

Price list for the Month of_____189__

A flyer from the store of George M. Brown at Cut Meat, South Dakota, on the Rosebud (Brule Sioux) Reservation, and dating after 1890, lists both the English and Lakota names for over 110 objects being sold, and their prices. The Lakota vocabulary was able to describe an amazing variety of objects that were totally unfamiliar to the Indians.

Many of these names were in use in pre-reservation times, and were lost as technology and reservation life evolved. Many of the Lakota names were not recorded by linguists and do not appear in standard Lakota-English dictionaries, or in the vocabulary of contemporary Lakota speakers.

This document proves that reservation educators were encouraging the Lakotas to read and write their language. It was only later, and then usually at the mixed tribe boarding schools, that students were punished for speaking in their native tongues. As well, it is an excellent reference to early reservation store stock for comparison to pre-reservation trade goods inventories of just 15 years earlier. The name of the community, Cut Meat, was later changed to Parmalee.

Allspice, Taspan opemnipi icahiye	60 to 30
Axle grease, Campagmiyan islaye	10
Axes, complete Mazunspe	1.25 to 1.00
Bacon, Kukuse sin	16 to 15
Baking powder, Winakapo	1¢ per oz.
Butcher knives, Mina ikceka	75 to 50
Burners, lamp, Petijanjan el maza ostanpi	5 to2 ½
Boots, Canhanpa iskahuhanska	5.00 to 3.00
Buttons, pearl, Ceskikan kogli	05
Buttons, china, Ceskikan ska	2½
Buttons, rubber, Ceskikan sapa	
Beads, seed, Psito iwaksu	15 to 10
Beads, brass, Psito maza	
Beads, necklace, Psito wanapin	
Bobs, ear, Swula	7½ to 5
Bowls, tin Maza wiyatke	
Brooms, owangicahinte	
Coffee, green, Pejuta sapa spansni [span]	15
Coffee, roasted, Pejutasapa spau	15
Crackers, Aguyapi saka	15 to 12½
Can goods, Maswoguake [maswognake]	10 to 35
Candies, Canhanpi hauska [hanska]	
Candles, Petijanjan ska	20 to 15

9

Cigarettes, Mnihuha cannupa kogapi [kagapi]	
Cheese, Asanpi wigli suta	25 to 15
Chocolate, Canha yukpanpi kalyapi	
Coffee pots, Wikalye	1.00 to 50
Cloves, Hi iyatinze	
Calicoes, Mnihuha ikceka	10 to 05
Cigarette paper, Mnihuha cannupa	
Canton flannel, Mnihuha okisehinsma	15 to 10
Cloth, blue, Sinato	2.00 to 1.85
Chidren's hose, Wakanheja tohunyakon [tahunyakon]	25 to 20
Combs, Nasunpakca	
Drawers, men's Mahel unzoge	75 to 40
Dried fruit, Taspa puza [taspan puza]	15 to 12½
Flour, Aguyopi blu [aguyagi blu]	2.25 to 2.00
Fish lines and hooks, Hoicuwa na maza	
Ginghams, Mnihuha can iyapehanpi	12½ to10
Goggles, Istamaza ogetonpi	
Hair pipes, Wawoslata	7½ to 5
Handerkerchief, silk, Wapahilate itipakinte	2.00 to 50
Handkerchief, cotton, Itipokinte ikceka [itipakinte ikceka]	15 to 10
Ham, Kukuse ceca ojutonpi	
Hats, men's, Wapostan wica tawa	4.00 to 2.00
Hats , boy's Wapostan hoksila tawa	2.50 to 1.00
Hoods, baby's, Hoksicala tawapostan	
Jumbles, Aguyapi skuya cokaya Ohiloka (sugared pastry) [ohloka]	20 to 15
Knobs, door, and lock, Tiyopa inatoke [inatake]	
Lye, Cahiota hanpi wispanye [cahota hanpi wispanye]	
Laundry blue, Itoye	
Lard, Wigli	5
Lamps, Petijanjan	
Lamp chimneys, Petijanjan janjan	25 to 15
Ladies' hose, Winyau tohunyakon [winyan tahunyakon]	
Matches, Yuwilepi	
Milk, condesed, Asanpi mas wognaka	
Mustard, btl., Wicahiyutapizi	
Macaroni, Wahanpi icahiye	
Muslin, bleached, Mnihuha ska zizipela	12 to 8
Muslin, unbleached, Mnihuha ska soka	10 to 7
Men's hose, Wica tahunyakon	15 to 6
Mosquito nets, capongwokeya	
Nails, Maswiyokatan	6 to 5
Nutmegs, Wastemna wicahi waspan yanpi	
Neckties, Tahuska inapin	50 to 25

10

Oatmeal, Wayahota yukpanpi	20 to 10
Oil, coal, Petijanjan wigli	35 to 30
Oil, cans, Petijanjan wigli iyokastan	60 to 40
Overalls, Akaul onzoge [akanl onzoge]	1.00 to 50
Pepper, black, Yamnumnugapi	10 to 8
Pickles, Wicohiyutapi toto [wicahiyutapi toto]	
Pants, Onzoge	2.00 to 1.00
Pans, dish, Waksica tanka80 to 50	
Plates, tin, Maswaksica	10 to 5
Pocket knives, Mina yuksijapi	2.00 to 50
Pocket books, Mazaska ojaha [ojuha]	40 to 30
Rice, Psin10 to 5	
Raisins, Canwiyapehe [cunwiyapehe]	15 to 10
Ropes, Hahionta wikon [hahonta wikan]	25 to 15
Sugar, Canhanpi ska	12# for 1.00
Salt, Mniskuya	3# sack for 10¢
Soap, laundry, Haipajaja onwojajapi	5
Soap, toilet, Haipajaja iglujajapi	5
Soda, Winakapo zi	
Starch, corn, Wipatinye sponyanpi [spanyanpi]	10 to 7
Starch, gloss, Ogle ipatinye [wipatinye]	10 to 6
Sardines, Hogan maswognaka blaska	25 to 15
Syrup, Tuhimaga canhanpi [tuhmaga canhanpi]	80 to 70
Shears, Iynsila [iyuhla]	25 to 15
Shawls, Sinahaswupi	2.00 to 1.00
Suits, men's, Wica hayapi	12.00 to 5.00
Suits, boys', Hoksila hayapi	5.00 to 2.50
Shoes, men's, Wica tacanhanpa	2.50 to .50
Shoes, ladies' Winyan tacanhanpa	2.50 to 1.00
Shoes, boy's, Hoksila tacanhanpa	2.00 to 1.00
Shoes, children's, Hoksicala tacanhanpa	1.50 to 75
Tea, Wahipa kalyapi [wa hpe kalyapi]	60 to 40
Tobacco, smoking, Canli yukpanpi	
Tobacco, chewing, Canli ikceka	
Table knives and forks, Mina na wicape	
Thread, cotton, Hahionta wicagege ikceka [hahonta]	
Thread, silk, Hahionta wicagege wapahilate [hahonta]	
Towels, Iteipakinte	25 to 15
Wash tubs, Kokawoyujaja	
Wash boards, Wipaskiskite	
Blankets	2.00 to 1.00
Wool Blankets	6.00 to 4.00

11

Beef issue day at Cut Meat Creek. Photos by John Anderson. c. 1893.
History Nebraska Collection.

Slaughterhouse at Cut Meat Creek. Photos by John Anderson, c. 1893.
History Nebraska Collection.

George Brown family on their Cody ranch on the South Dakota/Nebraska border, c. 1902
George is in the wagon with his daughter, little Susie.
Left to right: George Jr., Joe, Jennie, Susie (Rooks) Brown, toddler Anita, Joseph Rooks, Sr.
Notice the tipis in the upper left corner.

Sometime around 1906, George sold the trading post, and the family moved into the wild and beautiful badlands area known as Red Stone Basin, south of the White River in what is now Jackson County, South Dakota. There, he operated a horse and cattle ranch which eventually grew to include a relatively large number of animals. This was in the free-range era before many fences existed, and the country was exceptionally wild, with an abundance of gray wolves, bobcats, and pumas around to prey on the stock. George branded his stock with a spade on the left shoulder, and the high quality of his horses was well-known throughout the general area.

George was an excellent horseman and was especially adept at breaking and training wild horses. Ever the showman, he was called upon to furnish show horses and bucking broncs for fairs and rodeos, which were beginning to become quite popular in western South Dakota.

He owned an old stagecoach, salvaged from an earlier day when it undoubtedly had seen service as a public conveyance in pre-railroad times. He would appear in local parades, driving the coach pulled by six well-trained horses.

My mother must have been about three years old when her family moved to Red Stone Basin ranch. The new home consisted of a primitive cave-like structure located near a spring. Although it lacked virtually all known comforts and conveniences, the family was happy there, as long as they could be together, and was perfectly satisfied with and well-adapted to near wilderness existence. Although the vegetation was sparse, with abundant cacti, sagebrush, and soapweed, there was good grazing for livestock in many places and shelter from wind and snow in winter. When allotments were given to American Indian families a little later, the Brown estates were situated about 18 miles south, near the present-day Bauman ranch. Some of the Brown children, including my mother, received allotments within Red Stone Basin itself, but the land there was regarded as suitable only for grazing as it was primarily badlands terrain.

George Brown family portrait c. 1904 in Rapid City, SD
Left to Right: Jennie, George Jr., Joe, George Sr., Back: Susie holding baby Leona.

RAPID CITY INDIAN BOARDING SCHOOL

The Browns valued education, perhaps as a consequence of George's early exposure at Carlisle Institute, and wanted each of their children to attend school for as long as possible. The best, most convenient, and most appropriate means of providing this benefit for their children was to send them to Rapid City, about 125 miles away, to attend the boarding school for American Indian Children operated by the U.S. Indian Service. This school accepted children in grades kindergarten through 8th grade and was run like a military academy, with uniforms, strict discipline, drilling, and marching to the cadence of a snare drum, and was located a couple of miles west of the city. When they reached six years of age, each of the Brown children was taken by train to the Rapid City Indian School and turned over to authorities there to be housed, educated, and cared for nine months of each year. My mother attended this school for seven years until graduating from the 8th grade. In addition to basic academic subjects, the students were taught vocational and homemaking skills, and most emerged better qualified to deal with life's ordinary demands and trials than the average young person of that day, owing to the practicality of that teaching.

The Brown sisters at Rapid City Indian Boarding School c. 1915/1916.
Leona is on the far right in a white dress.

1

Pupils enrolled in................Rapid City................nonreservation
school during fiscal year ending June 30, current fiscal year.

Name	Tribe	Superintendency, or when unknown, give post office, county, and State
Adams, Benjamin	Sioux	Pine Ridge
Poyer, Mitchell	"	"
" Sam	"	"
" James	"	"
Battle, Daniel	"	"
Brave Heart, Moses	"	"
Brings Yellow, James	"	"
" Charles	"	"
Brown, Joseph	"	"
" Susie	"	"
" Anita	"	"
" Leona	"	"
" Rosa	"	"
" Angelic	"	"
" Louise	"	"
" Rosie	"	"
" Florence	"	"
Battleyoun, Rena	"	"
Badger, Sallie	"	"
Poyer, Ida	"	"
Battleyoun, Mary	"	"

Rapid City Indian School Enrollment 1913

U. S. Indian School, Rapid City, S. D.

Pupils enrolled in ___ school during current fiscal year. ___ nonreservation

NAME. (Group pupils by reservations.)	TRIBE.	SUPERINTENDENCY, OR WHEN UNKNOWN, GIVE POST OFFICE, COUNTY, AND STATE.
Pouillard, Isaac	Sioux	Pine Ridge
Richards, Charles	"	" "
" , Antoine	"	" "
Russel, Albert	"	" "
Swallow, Daniel	"	" "
" , Charles	"	" "
Skilander, Fred	"	" "
Tappio, Raymond	"	" "
" , Richard	"	" "
Twiss, Wallace	"	" "
" , Paul	"	" "
" , Charles	"	" "
Wounder Head, Peter	"	" "
White , Martin	"	" "
White, Sam	"	" "
Wilde, Charles	"	" "
Arrow Mound, Sallie	"	" "
Battleyoun, Mary	"	" "
Brown, Clorette	"	" "
" , Leona	"	" "
" , Jennie	"	" "
" , Louise	"	" "
" , Rose	"	" "
Big Boy, Emma	"	" "

Rapid City Indian School Enrollment 1916

Pupils enrolled in Rapid City Indian *nonreservation school during current fiscal year.*

NAME. (excep. pupils to reservations.)	TRIBE.	SUPERINTENDENCY, OR WHEN UNKNOWN GIVE POST OFFICE, COUNTY, AND STATE.	
Two Bulls, Moses	Sioux	Pine Ridge	
Two Bulls, Peter	Sioux	Pine Ridge	
White, Martin	Sioux	Pine Ridge	
Rounded, Denver	Sioux	Pine Ridge	
Rounded, William	Sioux	Pine Ridge	
Rounded Arrow, Harry	Sioux	Pine Ridge	
Rounded Bead, Peter	Sioux	Pine Ridge	
Wright, George	Sioux	Pine Ridge	
Yankton, Albert	Sioux	Pine Ridge	
Bear Robe, Julia	Sioux	Pine Ridge	
Black Bear, Jessie	Sioux	Pine Ridge	
Brave Eagle, Jessie	Sioux	Pine Ridge	
Breast, Stella	Sioux	Pine Ridge	
~~Broken Leg, Emma~~	~~Sioux~~	~~Pine Ridge~~	
Brown, Clorette	Sioux	Pine Ridge	
Brown, Helen	Sioux	Pine Ridge	
Brown, Isabelle	Sioux	Pine Ridge	
Brown, Leona	Sioux	Pine Ridge	
Brown, Louise	Sioux	Pine Ridge	
Brown, Pansy	Sioux	Pine Ridge	
Cedar, Susie	Sioux	Pine Ridge	
Chief Eagle, Annie	Sioux	Pine Ridge	
Chips, Susie	Sioux	Pine Ridge	
Clifford, Alice	Sioux	Pine Ridge	
Clifford, Emma	Sioux	Pine Ridge	
Clifford, Esther	Sioux	Pine Ridge	
Clifford, Grace	Sioux	Pine Ridge	
Clifford, Hattie	Sioux	Pine Ridge	
Clifford, Louise	Sioux	Pine Ridge	
Clifford, Mary	Sioux	Pine Ridge	
Clifford, Sybil	Sioux	Pine Ridge	
Craven, Agnes	Sioux	Pine Ridge	
Craven, Hazel	Sioux	Pine Ridge	
Craven, Minnie	Sioux	Pine Ridge	
Crow, Dora	Sioux	Pine Ridge	
Cuney, Eva	Sioux	Pine Ridge	
Galligo, Mary	Sioux	Pine Ridge	
Galligo, Lucy	Sioux	Pine Ridge	
~~Garnet,~~ Garnet, Edith	Sioux	Pine Ridge	
Garnet, Olive	Sioux	Pine Ridge	
Gerry, Mary	Sioux	Pine Ridge	
Good Elk, Lucy	Sioux	Pine Ridge	
Harvey, Emma	Sioux	Pine Ridge	
Harvey, Mary	Sioux	Pine Ridge	
Helper, Lucy	Sioux	Pine Ridge	
Hunter, Cornelia	Sioux	Pine Ridge	
Iron Teeth, Louise	Sioux	Pine Ridge	
Iron Teeth, Nancy	Sioux	Pine Ridge	
Iron Teeth, Rose	Sioux	Pine Ridge	
Jacobs, Celestia	Sioux	Pine Ridge	
Jelouis, Fannie	Sioux	Pine Ridge	
Jensen, Alice	Sioux	Pine Ridge	
King, Helen	Sioux	Pine Ridge	

Rapid City Indian School Enrollment 1918

Pupils enrolled in _____ *nonreservation*

school during current fiscal year.

NAME. (Group pupils by reservations.)	TRIBE. Sioux	SUPERINTENDENCY, OR WHEN UNKNOWN, GIVE POST OFFICE, COUNTY, AND STATE. Pine Ridge
1. Bissonette, Lottie	"	"
2. Black Bear, Rosa	"	"
3. Breast, Stella	"	"
4. Brown, Gloretta	"	"
5. " , Isabel	"	"
6. " , Jennie	"	"
7. " , Helen	"	"
8. " , Leona	"	"
9. Cedar, Susie	"	"
10. Chief, Nancy	"	"
11. Cuney, Eva	"	"
12. Craven, Minnie	"	"
13. Clifford, Alice	"	"
14. Clifford, Hattie	"	"
15. " , Mary	"	"
16. " , Sibyl	"	"
17. Goings, Leta	"	"
18. Helper , Martha	"	"
19. " , Lucy	"	"
20. Hunter, Cornelia	"	"
21. Iron Plume, Emma	"	"
22. " " , Hanna	"	"
23. Jacobs, Caroline	"	"
24. " , Celestia	"	"
25. " , Rosa	"	"
26. Janis, Dorothy	"	"
27. Jelouis, Fannie	"	"
28. Lebuff, Idaline	"	"
29. " , Jeanette	"	"
30. Little Bald Eagle, Jessie	"	"
31 " " " , Rosie	"	"
32. Lipps, Rosa	"	"
33. Logan, Ida	"	"
34. " , Nancy	"	"
35. Long Horn, Lizzie	"	"
36. Means, Ada	"	"
37. O'Rourke, Isabel	"	"
38. " , Louise	"	"
39. Peano , Delila	"	"
40. Quiver, Julia	"	"
41. Runs Along the Edge, Alice	"	"
42. Red Eyes, Maggie	"	"
43. Ruff, Alberta	"	"
44. " , Emma	"	"
45. Running Bear, Hattie	"	"
46. Turning Holy, Elizabeth	"	"
47. Thunder Bull, Cora	"	"
48. " " , Mabel	"	"

Rapid City Indian School Enrollment 1919

34

DEPARTMENT OF THE INTERIOR
UNITED STATES INDIAN SERVICE
RAPID CITY, S. D.   Oct. 30, 1920.

To Parents of Indian Children in Rapid City:

I observe that there are a number of Indian children
in the city and around the camps who are not attending any
school. I shall be obliged to take some very strong
measures to see that all such children attend school un-
less you do something very soon. If these children belong
on the reservations and are to attend the reservation
schools, you should take them home immediately. If you
intend to live here and wish to have your children in the
public school in the city, you should place them there at
once. If you can do neither of these ways, you must bring
your children here to this school, or if you have come
into town for the purpose of sending your children here
you should report at the office at once. All children of
school age must be taken care of during the coming week,
and if necessary I shall call upon the city authorities to
enforce this order. Let's have not unpleasantness about
this but everybody get into school which is the best thing
for all.

Yours truly,

_____
Superintendent.

Letter from the Department of the Interior to the Parents of Indian Children, 1920.

PART TWO

Pine Ridge Indian Boarding School

Manuscript by Sylvan Hauff

Compiled and edited by Tracy Hauff

PINE RIDGE INDIAN BOARDING SCHOOL

My mother, Leona Mattie Brown, like all members of her family, including her parents, was a diminutive woman, about 5' 3" tall, and usually weighed around 125 pounds. She had dark brown eyes and very dark brown hair. Her complexion and physical characteristics reflected her Lakota ancestry to some extent. She was intelligent, well-spoken, and very pleasant in all her contact with others, but by nature was a quiet, introspective person who kept busy with domestic chores and, in general, minded her own business. She was an excellent cook, baker, seamstress, and housekeeper. If opposites attract one another, she and William were very well suited as marriage partners, though it is questionable how well they communicated or understood one another. Throughout most of their marriage, William referred to her as "Leo," but no one else used this nickname. We children all called her "Mom" and loved her dearly. Her children were the central focus of her life, and she gave everything she had to ensure their well-being.

As a child of 5 or 6, Leona developed rheumatic fever, which damaged the mitral valve in her heart. Although she recovered from the fever and was robust, strong, and active throughout the balance of her childhood and early adult years, the physical strain of bearing five children and carrying the heavy burden which was the lot of the typical ranch wife in those days, proved too much for her. In 1938, Leona began to experience the unmistakable symptoms of cardiac deficiency. The government doctor who came to the clinic at Wanblee diagnosed her disorder and offered his grim prognosis, counseling against any continuation of her rigorous domestic activities. She was 35 years old and had 4 children under 13 years of age. I was 9 years old.

I have mentioned that my parents' small ranch was located in a remote area, far from any roads or town. There were no schools anywhere within 10-12 miles and no prospects that any would be built in the foreseeable future. It was apparently a foregone conclusion that, when the time came, we children would be sent away to the government boarding school for Indian children at Pine Ridge, some 120 miles from home. The precedence for such a school placement had been established and pursued in my mother's family much earlier, and under the circumstances, it was the only logical solution if we children were to have any kind of education. Both of my parents were firm believers in education as the means to a successful and happy life and often spoke of their hope that we would take every advantage of whatever educational opportunities were open to us. At home, with no outside informational sources or distractions, such as radio, television, newspapers, or regular and informed visitors available to us, we were obliged to depend on each other for communication, entertainment, and the sharing of feelings and information.

During our early childhood, I think, in some respects, the situation in our home must have resembled that prevailing even today during certain conservative religious groups, which deliberately and purposefully limit or eliminate all unwanted sources of outside information to protect their members from undesirable worldly influences. I think particularly of the Amish, Hutterite, and other such groups. However, such restricted or rigidly structured exposure to the outside world was never a part of my parents' child-rearing practices or goals.

My father had been to Europe, had seen gay Paris and some of the large cities, and was considered more socially sophisticated than the average cattle rancher or farmer of his day. He was inclined to speak to his children often and at great length, frequently addressing them as he would an adult. He was a verbal thinker who enjoyed hearing himself talk, and he consciously or unconsciously sought to impress his audience with the breadth of his knowledge on diverse subjects. As small children, we were kept abreast of current political and social developments, fed constant commentary on various topics, and encouraged to think for ourselves. At first, these topics centered around farming and ranching, but after we acquired our first radio and began receiving the Sunday edition of the Denver Post and another weekly newspaper, the topics for Dad's lectures ranged far and wide. I recall that our infrequent adult visitors were treated to much of my father's rhetoric and discussion, and they all seemed to appreciate his views and expostulations, if not his firmly held opinions. My mother listened but did not involve herself in lengthy, weighty discussions of world affairs. Her world was her home and her children.

In 1935, my older brothers, Billie and Dick, who were 9 and 7 years old respectively, were taken to Pine Ridge and enrolled in the large boarding school. About 600 children in grades kindergarten through 12th attended this school and lived together in dormitories in groups of various ages. The children remained at the school from early September until Christmas when they were allowed a 2-week vacation with their families. In early January, they returned to school and remained there through early May, when they were released to spend 3 ½ glorious months at home.

The Oglala Community School at Pine Ridge was located ½ mile west of the village of Pine Ridge, where the Bureau of Indian Affairs (BIA) headquarters was located, and resembled a small college campus, with many large red brick buildings, all constructed according to prescribed BIA designs. There were green lawns and trees, cement sidewalks with steel railings, and a large powerhouse with a tall brick chimney belching giant clouds of smelly black coal smoke. The school was designed to be as self-sufficient as possible and had its own laundry, bakery, dairy barn, horse barn, root cellar, and irrigated vegetable gardens. It also had an extensive swine production unit, poultry house, and large beef herd. Practically all the food consumed by the children was produced on-site. The BIA employed all instructional and administrative staff, and the entire operation had the distinctive look and imprimatur of a U.S. government installation. The BIA operated many similar boarding schools in many different states, and in 1935, there were at least seven such schools operating in South Dakota, including schools at Rapid City and Flandreau.

I was 6 years old when I entered boarding school in the fall of 1936 and began kindergarten. Although I should have been in first grade, I was small for my age and placed with those nearer my size. While I can recall no particular initial distress at having to leave my home and parents and enter an utterly alien world, my older brothers having gone there the previous year and continuing with me, the novelty soon wore off, and life as a boarding school student became unbearably lonely and hard.

#3647 U.S. School for Indians at Pine Ridge, South Dakota.
John C. H. Grabill Collection, 1891

Pine Ridge Indian Boarding School. Photo by Sylvan Hauff c. 1946

Many of the structural components of a military system still existed in 1935, and many of the staff members who wanted their secure government positions until retirement were on board for military academy practices. The rules of student behavior were strict, and students were expected to take care of themselves and perform all prescribed work, academic and personal care functions according to a rigid time frame.

A loud steam whistle at the power plant awakened everyone at 6:00 a.m., after which everyone was expected to rise immediately, dress themselves, make their beds, and wash up. At 6:30, a bell rang in the dining room, signaling everyone to line up according to grade and proceed into the dining hall for breakfast. Boys were seated at the north end of the hall, while girls were in the south end. Feeding was cafeteria style, and the food was simple but ample, and each student received the same amount of food on his tray. At 7:30, everyone began his assigned work detail, which involved cleaning and straightening up dormitory areas, carrying out trash containers, policing up the surrounding lawns, etc. By 8:00, everyone was dressed for school and in their classroom, where they remained until 11:00 a.m., at which time all elementary students were let out for lunch. High school students had lunch at 11:30 a.m., and classes resumed at 1:00 p.m. The steam whistle at the power plant signaled each of these events. At 4:00 p.m., classes ceased, and students returned to their dormitories except those involved in athletics or band. These latter students practiced their activities until 5:00 p.m. At 5:30, dinner was served, and after that, most of the students stayed in their dorm and did their homework, or, if they had none, were free to play or loaf until bedtime, which was 7:30 p.m. for those in kindergarten through 8th grade, and 9:30 for those in high school.

Upon arrival at school in the fall, each child was issued two sets of clothing, one for school and one for play, including a single pair of high-top leather shoes, a warm jacket, and a stocking cap. Each item was indelibly marked with the individual's assigned box number in heavy, black, waterproof ink. I can still smell the acrid aroma of this ink, which permeated all parts of the large boy's dormitory building and seemed to linger through Christmas each year.

A ritual for all younger boys in the fall was the fine combing of their hair and dousing the hair in kerosene to kill head lice and nits, which many of the children carried to school. I am still amazed that in my 13 years as a student there, I never acquired these unwelcome pests, but I was subjected to the fine-combing ritual at regular intervals until about the 4th grade, as were all the other little boys at the beginning of each school year.

Photo taken by Sylvan Hauff of the younger boys at Pine Ridge Indian Boarding School. c. 1946

Life in an all-Indian boarding school was not easy for a boy who was 3/16 Oglala Lakota and small for his age. There were the inevitable pecking order disputes, the fights to determine one's rank in the order, the constant testing and trials among the boys, the assertion of authority, and the domineering abuse levied upon weaker boys by more aggressive ones. Many of these boys were born fighters from large families where they learned to fight and walk simultaneously. There were always a number of bullies who gathered a gang of followers around themselves and made life miserable for those who refused to grant them obeisance and turn over their possessions or perform menial services for them. The gang would often attack a boy at the request of their leader, and while there were few serious injuries, there were many black eyes and split lips. For protection, the full-blood boys and the Ieska (mixed-blood) generally kept to their respective groups.

My parents were unable to visit us at school, and we got to see them only at Christmas and during the summer months, and there were times when parental affection and attention were sorely needed. My only consolation during these difficult times was that most of my schoolmates were suffering the same pangs of loneliness and homesickness but were equally restrained from expressing or displaying any signs of weakness. I recall hearing my mother speak with special fondness about a few chums she had at the Rapid City Indian School, and I came to realize how valuable and sustaining such friendships can be when one is separated from his family for long periods. It often seemed that there was no end to the days left before Christmas vacation and that the school year would never end. Once it did end, I always faced the necessity of returning to school at the end of the vacation period and tried my best to defer the thought of this unpleasant but inevitable eventuality.

Gradually, I accepted the relative harshness, rigidity, and regimentation of boarding school life. Many years later, while employed as a federal probation and parole officer, I had the occasion to visit several different federal prisons and reformatories and was struck by the similarities between inmate life and the life I had led for many years as a child. Institutional living, with or without barred windows and doors, is the same in many respects. I vowed never to submit my children to boarding school dehumanizing circumstances, but in more recent years, and upon mature reflection, I realize that there are far worse circumstances in the world and that, in many respects, I was fortunate to have experienced these early agonies. I even have some very pleasant recollections of the camaraderie that existed and the many activities we participated in. Adversity can be a good teacher, provided one survives the ordeal, which most of us did.

I often wonder what my life would have been like without the early boarding school experiences. I do not think it would have been nearly as rosy as I once imagined, and I no longer harbor any resentment toward my parents for having inflicted such undeserved punishment on me. I now agree that what must have been an equally painful and agonizing decision and ordeal for them was in my best interest and represented a display of uncompromising devotion and tough love on their part. To have done otherwise would have led us to a life of stagnation, ignorance, and mischief, given what I have come to recognize as my natural proclivities.

Boarding school students were allowed to go downtown, to the small village of Pine Ridge, for 2 hours on Saturday afternoon, provided they had money to spend and had not committed some infraction during the week resulting in their being "campused." All students were required to attend services at the church of their choice on Sunday morning. Every little boy was fitted with a nicely tailored wool suit, white shirt, and necktie, which were to be worn only to church. I learned many years later that the suits and shoes issued to us were made by inmates at the Federal Penitentiary in Leavenworth, Kansas. Religion instruction was also mandatory for one hour a week in the classroom.

My siblings and I had all been baptized in the Evangelical Lutheran Church early in life, which was my father's church. There was no Lutheran Church at Pine Ridge, so we all chose to attend our mother's Episcopal Church. Eventually, each of us was confirmed in this faith, and all of us adhered more or less to the tenets of the Episcopal Church during our lifetimes. Episcopal membership is one of the things that held us together as a family and provided a common thread of belief and values which we all came to share, some more than others.

The almost diametric opposition that seemed to characterize the personalities of my parents and result in a union entirely dominated by my father and my mother's almost complete subjugation, I believe, led to much unhappiness on the part of both, caused each of their children to reflect with mixed feelings, each in his own way, as to the efficacy of such a union, and perhaps to conclude at times that these two should never have married, or that each would have been happier married to someone more like themselves. It can probably be deduced from their subsequent marital choices that each of their children sensed a certain loss and regret in this relationship and was determined not to make the same mistake in their own choice of mates.

Each of the boys, Billie, Dick, and I, chose a strong-willed and self-reliant wife who was not about to allow herself to be pushed around, quite unlike their mother, while our sister, Luella, chose an easygoing, thoroughly down-to-earth husband, entirely unlike her father. These unions proved stable and enduring and have shown few of the tensions, uncertainties, apprehension, and anxieties that seemed to characterize their parent's union. As their child, one who always felt loved and cared for by both of them and who loved and cared for each of them with equal ardor, I do not think that I am doing a disservice to my parents' memory by criticizing their choice of marital partners. As an early, somewhat objective but not entirely unbiased observer of their relationship and a product/beneficiary/victim of their union, I must honestly and respectfully attest to having witnessed a great deal of unhappiness and pain which might have been averted had each chosen someone more like themselves. Being the thoroughly honorable people that they were, neither ever seriously considered ending the relationship, and they never openly quarreled or criticized each other in our presence at any time.

When I entered the Oglala Community boarding school at Pine Ridge in the fall of 1936, the children there were predominantly American Indian, many of whom could not speak English when they started school, but there was also a significant number who, like me, were part white. I had not been taught to think of myself as an Indian person and was initially somewhat shocked to find myself in an ocean of little brown bodies during our first mass showering. Any semblances of individualization were soon eradicated when we were all issued identical clothing, herded into groups according to grades, and subjected to a series of indisputable rules of behavior and unbiased punishment for infractions of the same. Through such commands and trial and error, we learned to conform our behavior to the rules, and most of us came to enjoy camaraderie and social interaction with our peers once we learned our place in the hierarchy. But there were many times when loneliness and yearning for our mothers' soothing love and care and the familiarity and comforts of home became overpowering. No particular effort was made on the part of the overseeing matrons and teachers to assuage such feelings or dry the copious tears, and we soon learned that not only would such a display of despair avail us nothing in the way of relief but was apt to invite the scorn and ridicule of our peers, many of whom delighted in tormenting their grieving companions. We learned to cancel our feelings and to compensate for them by building an effective emotional shield about ourselves that did not allow us to think about home or family. The advice I received from my parents and siblings concerning conflicts that inevitably arose at school was to "fight your own battles." I interpreted this to mean, "Don't expect anyone in your family to come to your rescue if you get into trouble." And no one ever came to my rescue.

As a light-skinned Ieska in an all-Indian boarding school, I was subjected to many early challenges by my darker-hued companions to establish who was to "rule the roost." I did not shirk from these encounters and came to be known as one who would stand his ground and defend himself. Eventually, I earned the right to be left alone and the nickname "Tuffy Hauff." When I got a little older, I joined the boxing team, where my pugilistic reputation grew to a certain extent. At first, I enjoyed this fearsome status and came to be something of a bully away from my family in a degree of social isolation, and I had very few friends except for those who sought my protection and leadership. At that point I resolved to stop flaunting my pugilistic talents and to avoid fights as much as possible, but I never completely shed my robe of self-defensiveness or my reputation as a fighter. Most of my fellow students seemed to respect and even fear me, and a few agreed to cultivate my friendship, perhaps to benefit from whatever protection or influence such friendship might afford.

I never felt welcome or comfortable throughout my thirteen-year stay at the boarding school. The physical plant and many rules of conduct became very familiar and less demeaning, and I liked and respected most of my teachers. But I could not change or increase the limited extent of my American Indian blood, and this was always a bone of contention. I was constantly reminded that because I did not meet the blood quantum standard set by the Bureau of Indian Affairs, I probably should not have been there and was essentially an interloper. The insecurity engendered by this situation had the effect of causing me to be particularly careful to obey all rules and avoid all possible conflicts, since it would not be difficult to justify my expulsion. I kept the lowest possible profile consistent with an excellent academic standard and was always academically at the top of my class.

I was raised in an artificial atmosphere of rather strict gender separation and was never comfortable around females until I completed college and a stint in the Army and got married. In boarding school, I had always lived in exclusively male dormitories, where any interaction with females, other than in the classroom, was severely restricted. Girls and boys were required to remain on their own sides of the campus after school hours and even to eat their meals separately. Most of us boys did not know how to behave around girls and did everything we could to avoid being teased for any actual or imagined romantic involvement. High school students inevitably formed romantic liaisons with girls, but these were usually limited to casual strolls in prescribed areas of the campus during broad daylight and under the watchful and seemingly hostile gaze of the very strict girls' matrons. Couples were allowed to sit together during weekly movies and, in the darkened theater, surreptitiously engaged in innocent hand holding and cuddling. The authorities were not totally devoid of an appreciation for natural feelings, which, in any event, were irrepressible.

I think I was about eleven years old when I first became aware of the presence and unusual attraction of Margaret Skalinder, a very pretty girl who was a year younger than me but a year ahead of me in school. She and her two older sisters, Essie and Mary Ann, younger sister, CeCee, and older brother, Sky, lived in a remote area northwest of Martin, South Dakota. Margaret had long dark hair, beautiful green eyes, and two of the prettiest dimples I have ever seen.

One day, a mutual friend, Marion Janis, approached me in the dining room and confided that Margaret liked me and wanted to sit with me at the Saturday night movie. I am certain that Marion had not been asked to convey this message to me, nor could she have known the profound and far-reaching impact and lasting effect that her message would bring, and I doubt that Marion would have any recollection of the event today, but bless her heart, she set in motion some wheels which have not stopped turning in my heart and will not stop until my life ends.

Some people seem to be made for each other, and if lucky enough to make a connection early in life, and if many other uncontrollable variables happen to click into place at the right time, and if God almighty wills it so, are destined at some point to share the crucial trials and felicities of life. I am not sure what it was that first attracted Margaret to me, or what was stirring in her 10-year-old heart, or in my own at the time. We shared many common experiences and attributes, including membership in the Episcopal Church, and were alike in many ways, but I found it difficult to believe that someone so lovely and sweet could possibly have a serious interest in me.

We were both shy, and when we were together had almost nothing to say to each other, but being together during the very brief and awkward moments allowed by the system that we were a part of carried a genuine thrill and excitement which is probably unique to very young lovers, at least it was for me.

For many blissful months, we sat together in the darkened movie theater and strolled the sidewalk near the old elementary school building after supper. We occasionally walked downtown together on Saturday afternoons and endured the inevitable teasing of our schoolmates.

Then, one day, Margaret's parents came to the school, and word quickly spread that she and her sister, Mary Ann, were leaving. I went to where their car was parked in time to see Margaret wave goodbye to me out of the rear window as they departed down the dusty road.

It was a time of great sadness for me, but then much of my life seemed filled with sadness in those early days of boarding school. I could not allow any outward show of grief or sorrow over the departure of my very first sweetheart, which would be perceived as a sign of weakness and vulnerability. Suppression of emotions had become a way of life for all of us at Pine Ridge, and we all developed our own technique for not letting things bother us. I did not allow Margaret's early departure and the very real prospect that I would never see her again bother me for very long, but I never forgot about her.

During the next seven years, we exchanged letters occasionally and saw each other very briefly at times, usually at football or basketball games when our schools competed, and somehow the spark remained alive in our hearts. It was always an incredible thrill for me to receive a letter from Margaret, catch a fleeting glimpse of her, or speak a few words with her, and I did not fail to notice that she was growing into a very beautiful and charming young lady! Her beauty was sure to attract a lot of attention wherever she went, and I never harbored any hope that she might one day be mine.

Margaret Skalinder at age 12.
This is the photo she gave to Sylvan when they attended Pine Ridge Indian Boarding School.
He carried it in his wallet his entire life.

8th grade class. Sylvan is sitting in the back under the arrow.

8th Grade class. Sylvan is leaning over the railing in the last row on the far right.

OCHS Glee Club, 1948. Sylvan is in the back row, fourth on the right.

Sylvan, perhaps 10th or 11th grade.

Sylvan, Quarterback, # 44. Middle row, center.

As time went by and I grew through adolescence into early adulthood, there were other brief romantic interludes with other girls, some more ardent than others, but none so important as to be worth mentioning here. I made a conscious effort to avoid serious involvement that could interfere with my hopes and dreams for a better life as an adult. While I had not formulated any definite plans as to what course I wanted my life to follow, I knew that I wanted to be self-reliant and, above all, to be free of the tangled web of dependency upon any form of government support or reliance which appeared to have ensnared and paralyzed so many of my Lakota contemporaries. I'm not sure where or when I first espoused the philosophy that has guided my life, for better or worse, from an early age. Perhaps it was at my parent's knees, or maybe it ran in the blood of my ancestors or developed spontaneously out of observations of the strangling effects of pathological dependency or the lives of Lakota persons who made the mistake of adhering too closely to the promises of the Federal Government regarding their slowly deteriorating culture. Perhaps the early resentment I felt at being dependent on the government boarding school for virtually every physical and social need while lacking full acceptance as an enrolled member of that society generated in me a determination to absolve myself of these connections once and for all, and as early as I could.

I have always realized that much was admirable in the old-time Lakota culture, different and strange though it was. There is much inherent good in those aspects of the culture, such as language, kinship patterns, and folkways. I can emphatically deny any sense of shame for my Lakota heritage. I am only thankful that circumstances and time allowed me to choose what world I wanted to live in and, in many ways, coerced my final choices.

Many people credit Franklin Roosevelt with ending the Great Depression and ushering in a new era of prosperity and peace with his New Deal philosophy of government. Nothing could be further from the truth. What the New Deal did bring about was a lot of government-funded programs to provide employment and economic relief to impoverished citizens, which, of course, was a godsend to many and ensured Mr. Roosevelt's reelection to four separate terms as president, but which fostered dependency and stopped self-reliance. The depression itself would linger until the entry of the United States into World War II. It was the wartime economy that changed the economic climate, not the New Deal. I believe that in time, the various recovery programs may have worked their intended purpose without a war; time alone is a great healer. But in 1940-41, we were still in the throes of the depression, and times were tough.

Because of my mother's health, we had to leave the ranch and move closer to civilization and a hospital. Although we children could spend only three months of summer there, we loved the ranch and hated to give it up. We loved the horses and cattle, our old dog Shep, and the familiar sights of the Badlands knobs and Medicine Butte in the distance. Living at the ranch was the happiest time of my childhood. Life was never the same for us after 1939 when we moved to a house my father owned in the tiny village of Parmelee on the Rosebud Indian Reservation. We children, except for our sister, Luella, still spent nine months each year at the Pine Ridge Indian Boarding School, even farther from our home than the ranch had been.

Concern for my mother's deteriorating health descended like a cloud on our family life and seemed to permeate our existence.

I know my hyperkinetic and ambitious father must have felt excruciatingly frustrated with the situation, and I can recall, even at 10 or 11 years of age, feeling very bad for both my parents and regretting being an additional burden to them. My older brother, Billie, then 15 years old, got a job as a pick and shovel laborer on the road building project on U.S. Highway 18, south of Parmelee, to help earn money for necessities. My father worked as a surveyor on a WPA-funded program sponsored by the South Dakota Department of Military Affairs. He made surveys and drew maps of the cemeteries in the area where military veterans were buried. My mother did her best to prepare our meals and wash our laundry to maintain some semblance of a normal home. My father took an interest in politics and began participating in Republican party affairs to a limited extent. Wendell Willkie was the Republican candidate against FDR, and Harlan Bushfield ran successfully for South Dakota governor.

Henry and Anna Hafner were my godparents and had always shown a special interest in me from an early age. During my summers at home from boarding school, I was often invited to spend several weeks with them and their family. Anna was my father's sister. The Hafner family always spoke German exclusively at home. They were always very kind to me and fed me liberally, and I enjoyed being with them. I understood that they wanted to help relieve the burden on my mother by taking at least one child off her hands temporarily. Still, at the same time, I felt ambivalent about using up much of my precious vacation days away from my own home and family.

In the summer of 1940, I went to Mt. Vernon, South Dakota, with the Hafners to spend the balance of the summer on their farm. They picked me up in Parmelee, and we traveled the 200 miles in their pickup. While I was at Mt. Vernon, my family moved from Parmelee to Rapid City, where my father had purchased a house next door to my grandparent's home at 623 Denver St. In early September, I was put aboard the train in Mitchell to travel to Rapid City to rejoin my family, and a few days later, I was taken back to Pine Ridge to resume school. I was eleven years old.

our home at Rapid

617 Denver Street, Rapid City, South Dakota.

Billie, Leona, Dick, Sylvan, and Luella at grandparent's house, 623 Denver St.

On December 7th, 1941, the Japanese suddenly attacked our military installations in Hawaii, and we were forced to open a Pacific theater of operations against that nation while continuing our war with Nazi Germany and Italy.

Early in 1942, my father enlisted in the U.S. Army and went to Camp Roberts, California, and later to Camp Bowie, Texas, for training. I am unsure to this day as to what his motivation was for leaving his sick wife and four children and going off to war, and I recall spending a lot of time agonizing over this matter while away at school. It was a time of great uncertainty and danger for Americans, and there were long lists of war casualties coming over the radio daily and word of many young men being killed in combat. The military draft was very active, and an eligible conscriptee could count on being summoned for duty on very short notice. High schools and colleges were emptying rapidly as young men were drafted or enlisted as soon as they reached their 18th birthday. But at age 41, my father was beyond draft age, and most men of his age, who were not in uniform, were leaving for West Coast cities to take well-paying jobs in defense plants.

A new Army Air Base was being established in Rapid City, and the shortage of manpower here and elsewhere created a heavy demand for workers of almost every type. The depression ended almost overnight, and new opportunities opened up, fueled by the nation's war effort. For those not of compulsory military service age or classified unfit for duty, this was to be a period of tremendous economic improvement. But not for my family. I know that my father agonized over his decision and afterward carefully explained to us that soldiering was the one thing he knew he could do well. He felt his duty to us and his country was to contribute to the army. What he said was true; he was an excellent soldier and soon was selected for Officer Candidate School and commissioned a Second Lieutenant. But his crucial vocational choice also led him into some of the most dangerous and intense combat of the war in Europe, where thousands of his comrades were killed or wounded, and for a considerable time, his family did not know if he was alive or dead, or if they would ever see him again.

Sylvan's writing ended here. I searched for notebooks, pads, or typed papers, hoping he had continued his story, but I did not find anything.

PART THREE

"Squaws" and "Squaw Men"

Joseph and Jennie (Adams McGaa) Brown

Joseph and Tiŋgleška (Bull Bear) Rooks

George and Susie (Rooks) Brown

William and Leona (Brown) Hauff

Sylvan and Margaret (Skalinder) Hauff

Manuscript by Tracy Hauff

"SQUAWS" AND "SQUAW MEN"

I believe it is important to discuss two terms that are used in this section - "squaw" and "squaw men." In the mid-to-late twentieth century, the word "squaw" was recognized as degrading and offensive, but the origin of the word is quite the opposite. The word was first documented in the 1600s and derived from the Algonquian word squáw or eskua. Other tribes who used this term included the Massachusetts - squá or ussqua, and the Chippewa - ikwé. All definitions meant woman and also signified female animals and plants. The different cognates eventually evolved into the ubiquitous word "squaw," and it began to be used to refer to all American Indian women regardless of tribe. The colonists who first settled in Massachusetts used the word squá when referring to strong female American Indian rulers who had a say in tribal dealings with white men.

By the 1800s, European colonists used "squaw" when referring to any reliable woman, white or Indian, and the Algonquian used it to refer to settler women who showed authoritative characteristics. The word soon became associated with productive, hardworking, responsible females. But this is when its meaning began a derogatory downhill slide. Because of its association with hard work, some plantation owners started to use it to refer to their female servants and slaves, thus placing a definitive lower-class socioeconomic inference on the word aimed at dehumanizing the women.

"Squaw" lost its true meaning and became a stereotype for women who had no social status and were not deserving of respect. Beaten and sexually abused by cruel white "owners," whether on a plantation or in one of the forts, this portrayal of "squaws" worsened until the detrimental false narrative behind all female American Indians became that of dirty, insignificant, morally corrupt women who held the lowest status in society.

The dark skin, eyes, and hair of both Indian and Black women were considered unattractive, indicating that the woman was a poor laborer with no rights. In contrast, the milky white skin of the plantation owners' wives became a symbol of affluence. The white news presses used racial descriptors when writing about Native women by inserting adjectives of color - black hair, black eyes, red skin, thus effectively removing them from the privileged white society. This disparaging determination of a person's worth and integrity based on skin color was carried into the American West by white men and women, and racial profiling was endorsed, placing Natives into a permanent underclass. Violence against Native women became synonymous with colonization. As immigration increased in the 1900s, this negative depiction was applied to other women with darker skin and brown eyes, such as Italian and Latino women.

The terms "squaw" and "squaw men" were used broadly and blatantly in the nineteenth century, and since I do not support erasing history (other than renaming historical landmarks that belonged to the Indigenous peoples before Euro-American encroachment, i.e., Harney Peak renamed to Black Elk Peak), I have used these terms as they were written. It is interesting to note that the Lakota tribes had always had a name for this distinctive summit before it was named Harney Peak. They called it Hinhan Gaha—Imitates Owl—because of the 360° view from the top, which is much like an owl turning its head all the way around.

Five of my great-great-grandfathers were white men known as "squaw men" because they chose Lakota women for their wives. According to historical and family accounts, these men acknowledged their marriages to their Native wives and were good fathers to their mixed-blood children. When the government ordered the removal of all Natives from Colorado, these husbands left with their wives and children, unlike some white men who sent their wives to the reservations and remained behind. The husbands did not refer to their wives as "squaws" but as "my wife, my woman, or the mother of my children."

JOSEPH AND JENNIE (ADAMS McGAA) BROWN

Joseph Carl Brown was born May 13, 1839, in Ohio. He arrived in Jefferson Territory (now Denver, Colorado) with the "Lawrence Party," a group of forty bold individuals who traveled from Lawrence, Kansas, to the Rocky Mountains to partake in the Pike's Peak Gold Rush. The men organized in Lawrence in the spring of 1858, began their journey west on May 19,1858, and arrived in Jefferson Territory that Fall.

"These Lawrence men who constituted what is known in the early annals of Denver as "the Lawrence Party," were men of action, for they completed their arrangements, got their wagons and draft animals, collected provisions, supplies, and tools for a season's operations, and started on their long journey on the 19th of May. Their company comprised Albert W. Archibald, A.F. Bercaw, Giles Blood, Frank Bowen, Joseph Brown, W.J. Boyer, William Chadsey, John Churchill, Frank Cobb… [etc.] ~ Smiley, Jerome C. History of Denver. The Times-Sun Publishing. ~

William McGaa, age thirty-five, and his attractive fifteen-year-old wife, Jennie Adams McGaa, were two of the first people Joseph met when he pitched his tent in the encampment of Indian Row along the banks of Cherry Creek. Jennie was half Wažaže Lakota and half white. Her captivating beauty was admired in the female-starved territory and has been recounted in several history books. McGaa never altered his origin story, saying he was born into a noble family in Scotland who owned a large estate called Glenarm. There was no way to verify his claim of nobility, but given his intelligence, Scottish accent, and business acumen, those who knew him did not doubt it. He introduced himself as "Jack Jones" when he first arrived in Colorado from Missouri, so it is fair to assume that he had done something shady back east that warranted an alias and quick relocation to the West. He continued to use Jack Jones whenever it suited him, but he signed all legal documents as William McGaa.

Indian Row Encampment

McGaa Cabin in Indian Row

Both sketches above were published in Smiley's 1901 book "History of Denver." They depict the first village on the confluence of Cherry Creek and South Platte River, which is currently Lower Downtown Denver (LoDo).

Mary Aŋpaha with her two brothers. In the center is Chief Aŋpaha of the Wažaže band, who lived with the Oglalas.

Jennie's mother, Aŋpaha Adams LaRocque, was born in 1830. One of the first things the Christian churches would do when they had prolonged contact with the Natives was give them an English Christian name. Along with hundreds of other young Native girls, the Catholic church gave Aŋpaha the name Mary, and she was known as Mary in her adult years.

Her tombstone reads that she was born in 1816, but I believe this is a misunderstanding as it is mentioned numerous times in historical documents that she was 13 years old in 1843 when she gave birth to her daughter, Jennie. This would mark her birth year as 1830. Also, if she had been born in 1816, she would have given birth to her daughter Louise at age 50, which was unlikely as women entered menopause earlier in the 1800s. I suggest that her first husband, John Alex Adams, was the one who was born in 1816.

In Lakota, aŋpa means daylight, and Aŋpaha translates to 'in daylight.' When used alone, paha translates to mound or hill, and I have seen the Lakota family name of Aŋpaha translated as Day Hill. This is incorrect. Paha can also mean 'to raise' or 'to strike.' Therefore, the correct translation of Aŋpaha would be 'to strike or raise daylight.' My sister Alison's middle name is Dawn. I never thought about it when we were young, but now I know why she was given this lovely name. In a couple of historical documents, I saw Aŋpaha written as Anputa. The Lakota word for day is aŋpetu, and Anputa must have been a mistranslation or misspelling because there is no such word as anputa in the Lakota language.

When Mary Aŋpaha first appeared in Colorado history, it was believed she was Arapaho, a member of the local Indigenous tribe. This mistake was corrected, and it was later documented that she was Oglala. Specifically, she was a member of the Wažaže band.

The Wažaže, or Water People, were one of the three original divisions that spoke the Dhegihan Sioux language, the other two being the Sky People and the Land People. The Osage, Ponca, Omaha, Quapaw, and Kansa (Kaw) lineages evolved from them. As a tribe of hunters and traders, they first lived in the Ohio River Valley before migrating west to the Mississippi River and crossing over to the Missouri River, following the river north. They met French fur traders along the Missouri and got along very well with them, beginning a trading collaboration that lasted from the 1700s through the 1800s. The constant pushing north and west by white settlers eventually brought them to the Titonwan tribes. Through intermarriages, they became a distinct band that lived among the Titonwans, primarily the Oglala and Sičangu.

Although it is unpleasant for us to think about today, in the 1800s, it was not unusual for an American Indian leader to give an unmarried female relative to a trapper or trader they respected, wishing to form a close alliance with these white men. These mixed-blood marriages were, for the most part, mutually beneficial relationships; the tribal leader received insider information and preferential trading, the white husband gained invaluable access to land, rivers, language, and cultural practices necessary for survival in the cutthroat business of the fur trade, and the women were respected as essential intermediaries. Some ruthless American Indian men did sell their sisters or daughters to obtain liquor or settle a gambling debt, and sadly, these Native women did not go to live with men of status and were not treated well by their white partners. It is known that Aŋpaha was given to the Platte River white trader, John Alex Adams, when she was only twelve, and in 1843, at age thirteen, she gave birth to their daughter Jennie at the fur outpost, Fort John, which later became the renowned Fort Laramie military post. When Adams passed away, Aŋpaha married a French-Canadian trapper, Alphonse LaRocque. Aŋpaha and LaRocque remained together until he died in 1877.

Mary Aŋpaha Adams LaRocque with grandson, Denver William McGaa.

Mary Aŋpaha Adams LaRocque in her later years. Digitized photo courtesy of History Colorado.

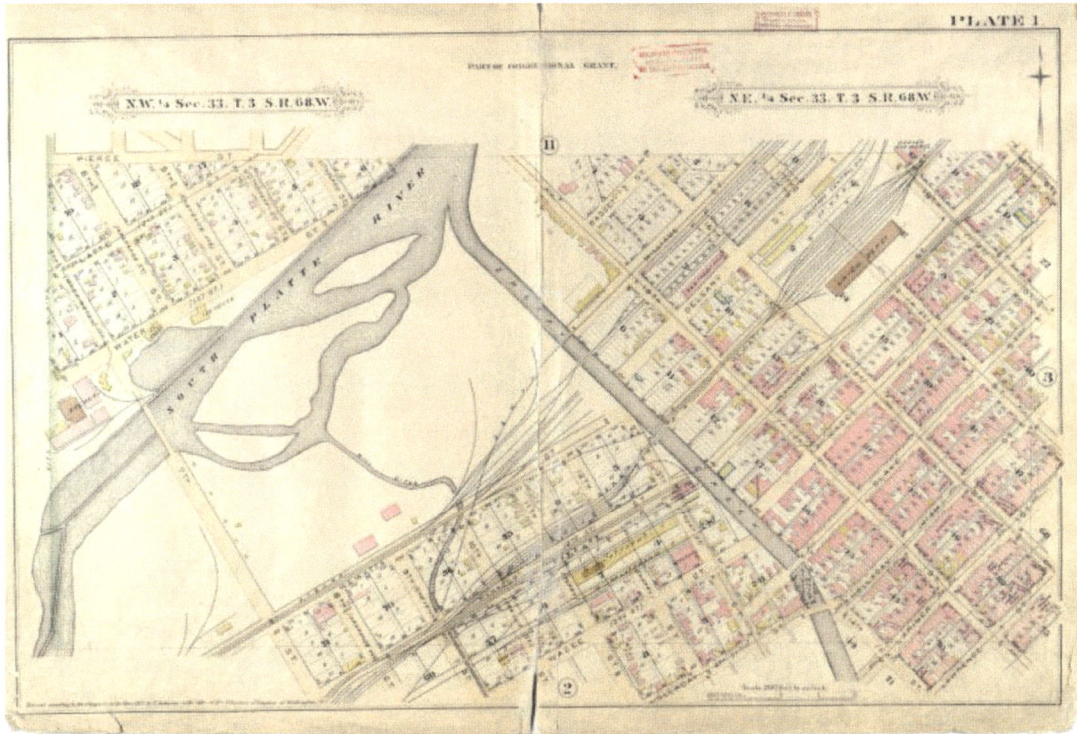

PLATE 1

Map of Auraria, "Denver's Oldest Neighborhood," at the South Platte River and Cherry Creek convergence. The map is courtesy of Denver Public Library Western History Collection.

Joseph Brown set about building a more permanent residence in the newly founded township of Auraria. The borders of Auraria form a perfect triangle that has not changed in over 160 years—Colfax Avenue on the south, the South Platte River to the west, and Cherry Creek designating the eastern border. The apex of the triangle is the point where the two rivers converge.

"As soon as the camp talk turned to the conclusion to organize a town company and lay out a town, they began cutting and preparing logs for a cabin, which they erected on what became the east side of Twelfth street, between Wazee and Wynkoop streets. Giles Blood, Joseph Brown, William Regan, and James White jointly started one a few days later and when the survey was finished it was found that these men in their hurry had got their cabin on the line of Twelfth Street between Wazee and Wynkoop; from which site it was later removed."

~ Smiley, Jerome C. History of Denver. The Times-Sun Publishing Company. 1901 ~

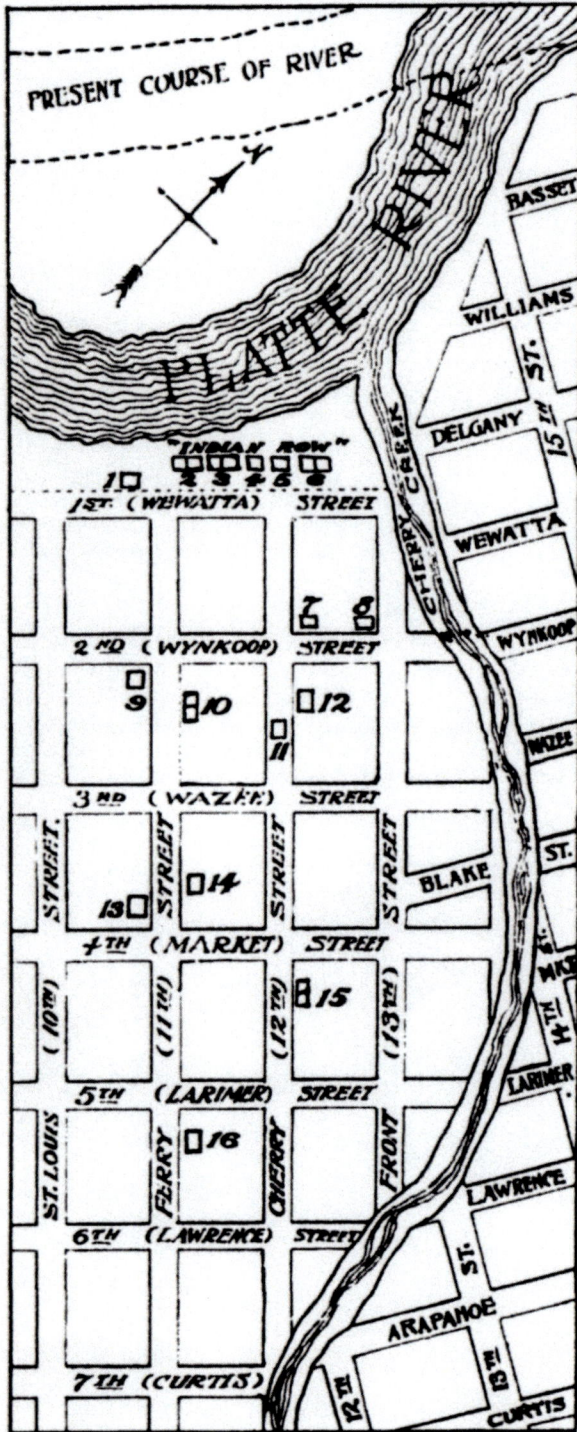

Number 11, shown in the middle of 12th Street, is the unfortunate placement of Joseph Brown's cabin with Blood, Regan, and White. Undaunted, Brown began construction on a new cabin, this time without any partners. McGaa's cabin is Number 3, shown in the original encampment of Indian Row.

McGaa named Wewatta Street for Jennie. The closest I came up with for a possible Lakota translation of this name is Wiya'ta (wee ya ta), meaning "at the sun." He supposedly named the street Wazee after Jennie, too. Wazi in Lakota means pine tree, but it also means "things that are yellow." The word zi (zee) used alone is the color yellow.

I have not read a single historical document that tried to make sense of the words Wewatta and Wazee. Historians were content in simply saying McGaa named the streets after his "squaw", and the meanings of the names were unimportant to them. I see the Lakota connection, even considering the mispronunciations, misinterpretations, and misspellings.

Wi is sun, zi is yellow (the color of the sun), and, as mentioned, the family name of Aŋpaha relates to the rising of the sun. The street names are definitely a tribute to Jennie's maternal Lakota lineage.

"In that first week of November 1858, preparations for building many other cabins in Auraria were under way. A.C. Wright was assigned a lot by the Town Company, on the northeast corner of Larimer and Tenth Streets. He cut and hauled logs for a cabin, and then traded the lot and logs to Joseph Brown for an old mare, and Brown later put up a house on that lot." ~ Smiley, Jerome. History of Denver. The Times-Sun Publishing Company. 1901. ~

On November 17, 1858, another township was platted across the creek. It was named Denver City.

Jennie and William's son, William Denver McGaa, was born here on March 8, 1859, and became quite famous as the first predominantly white baby born in Denver. His parents and the village called him Denver. His grandmother, Aŋpaha, called him Čaŋpá Wakpa, 'Cherry Creek.'

"At the mouth of Cherry Creek others who fancied prospecting and light dry air were calling a town Saint Charles, in honor of their home back in Missouri. William McGaa (alias Jack Jones), John Palmer and Joseph Brown lived on the banks of Cherry Creek enjoying wild game, their Sioux wives' wo-ja-pi made from the abundant choke cherries and doing a little prospecting. As more miners arrived, the town grew to 5,000 and the name was changed to Denver, honoring the fifth governor of Kansas Territory. When the McGaa's son was born, he was named William Denver McGaa and noted in History books as the first child of white blood born there." ~ Miller, Irma. French-Indian Families in America's West. Trafford Publishing. 1988. ~

On February 26, 1861, Colorado was declared a territory. President Abraham Lincoln appointed William Gilpin—a staunch Manifest Destiny advocate—as the first territorial governor. The McGaa family and Brown moved north this year to LaPorte (originally named Colona), Colorado. The new community, founded by the fur traders John Provost, Antoine Janis, and their Indian wives, had a population of 50 French-Indians. Jennie's mother, Aŋpaha, was already there with her husband, Alphonse LaRocque. Around five hundred Lakota and Arapaho were also living in the area. Racial discrimination had accompanied the multitude of white prospectors swarming into the newly established town of Denver, and the mixed-blood families soon realized that they were no longer welcome. LaPorte, with its sizeable French-Indian population, was to be their haven where they could live in harmony.

William and Jennie had a daughter, Jessie, in 1860 and another son, John, in 1862. Sometime in 1866, McGaa disappeared from LaPorte while on a trip to Denver. No one knew what had happened to him; he simply vanished. Almost a year passed with no word from William, and all who knew him presumed he was deceased.

After McGaa's disappearance, Joseph Brown began to court Jennie. She had known Brown almost as long as she had known McGaa. He had lived on Indian Row with them in the Cherry Creek village and, along with her husband, was one of the founders and stockholders of the Auraria Town Company. It seemed natural that Jennie should choose Joseph from among the many suitors in LaPorte who wanted to claim her as their wife.

The opposite of the flamboyant, ostentatious McGaa, Brown was a subdued man who preferred the solitude of mining, logging, and freighting. From time to time, he would trek up into the mountains in search of gold. It is unknown how much his expeditions yielded, but his primary source of income—freighting—kept him afloat in the new territory.

As suddenly as he had disappeared, McGaa reappeared in the fall of 1867 and was devastated when Jennie refused to take him back. Always an obnoxious drinker, he became particularly unruly after losing Jennie, and in December 1867, he was thrown in jail during one of his drunken binges. The only heat in the poorly ventilated building came from a faulty woodstove that became blocked, and carbon monoxide accumulated at a deadly level. William perished in his jail cell; the cause of death was determined to be suffocation.

The Rocky Mountain News published a benevolent obituary on December 16, 1867.

"Died, in this city, yesterday, in the morning, Dec 15, William W. McGaa, better known as "Jack Jones," in his 45th year. The deceased had been a resident of the Rocky Mountain regions about 28 years, the companion of Beckwourth, Bridger and other mountaineers of note. He was a man of more than ordinary intelligence, and a very fair education. Generous to a fault, and a steadfast friend. His remains were buried yesterday evening in Mt. Prospect Cemetery, followed by a few of the old friends who first knew him here in the spring of 1859. Peace to his Ashes."

Jennie Adams McGaa became Mrs. Joseph Brown on August 10, 1868. The couple was married in a double ceremony with Joseph Rooks and Ann Claymore (aka Tiŋgleška) on the Benjamin Lessert (aka Claymore) ranch in Larimer County, Colorado. Ranches served as marriage venues in those days, as a church would not be built in LaPorte until the 1870s. Little did these two couples know that in 23 years, their offspring, George Brown and Susie Rooks, would be married in South Dakota on the Pine Ridge Indian Reservation.

The marriage certificate of Joseph Brown and Jennie McGaa filed in Larimer County in 1868.

The marriage certificate of Joseph Rooks and Ann Claymore (Tiŋgleška) filed in Larimer County in 1868.

Jennie Adams McGaa Brown, c. 1875
Born 1843, Fort John, Wyoming
Died 1878, LaPorte, Colorado
Photo copyright 1996-2018, City of Fort Collins

The Browns were married for ten years and had three children. Joseph Carl Brown Jr. was born in 1869, George Racine Brown in 1871, and Jennie Brown Jr. in 1873. Unfortunately, there was no "happily ever after" in the marriage of Joseph and Jennie.

The first body buried in the LaPorte, Colorado, Bingham Hill cemetery in 1862 was nine-month-old Bazille Provost, son of French-Canadian fur trader John Provost and his Dakota wife, White Owl. Jennie's son, John McGaa, was buried there in 1867 at the young age of four. Jennie Brown was the ninth person buried in the cemetery in 1878. The cause of her death is controversial and tragic by all accounts. Some say she committed suicide, but even that story has two versions—one is that she poisoned herself, and the other is that she purposely walked into the Cache la Poudre River and drowned. Another variation of this is that it was an accidental drowning. The poisoning has been challenged because whenever there was a sudden mysterious death at that time, superstitious full and mixed-blood Indians attributed it to poisoning. The newspaper article, 'Denver's 'Denver': Friend of the Indians," went as far as to report, "Deeply depressed, Jennie Brown, at age 35, was dying from poison she had taken. By the time the doctor arrived, it was too late."

Jennie's son, Denver, said she drowned, and Denver's daughter, Hazel McGaa Cuney, said Jennie's death resulted from poisoning. Another version, one that I consider to be highly likely, came from Adele Brown Treis—the Brown family historian and genealogist—who believed Jennie accidentally poisoned herself while trying to terminate a pregnancy. The Native women knew which plants/herbs were abortifacients. I have contemplated the discrepancy in cause of death and believe that a plausible scenario could be that Jennie accidentally overdosed on a natural abortifacient, which would cause hemorrhaging, and walked into the river to cleanse herself where she could have lost consciousness or been swept away by the current. This is a feasible explanation for two very dissimilar causes of death. With conflicting stories told by family members and written by journalists, the actual cause of Jennie's death will remain a mystery.

Jennie Brown's grave, Bingham Hill Cemetery, LaPorte, Colorado.
Photos by Tracy Hauff, 2022.

Denver's 'Denver': Friend of the Indians

By SUSAN HALL

William Denver McGaa worked on the Pine Ridge Reservation in South Dakota and taught the Indians to farm and manage cattle.

ALTHOUGH HER LIFE was short, Jennie McGaa Brown, a beautiful half Oglala Sioux, gave a major historical contribution to Denver. She was destined to give birth to "Denver" McGaa, the first predominantly White child born in Denver.

Jennie was born in 1843 to John and Mary Adams. Her father was a White frontiersman and her mother a full-blooded Oglala Sioux. In the autumn of 1858, the family was living at Cherry Creek, where 15-year-old Jennie met and married William McGaa (often called Jack Jones), a mountain man, trapper and Indian trader.

McGaa was born in Great Britain of Scotch-Irish descent, the son of an English nobleman. He had run away from home at an early age and, because his father felt he had disgraced the family, he wasn't allowed to return. McGaa sailed to America and made his way west. Later, McGaa thought it would be a good idea to write his parents to see if they were still alive and to let them know he was prospering. When he wrote, he used his fictitious name of "Jack ," pretending to be the employer of a young man named McGaa. In time, a reply came from his father in England encouraging "Jack Jones" to persuade the "boy McGaa" to return home because his parents were getting old and wanted to see him. The father also noted that the boy would soon inherit the estate. He invited

"Jack Jones" to accompany his son and wrote that they would be well taken care of, lacking nothing. It isn't known if McGaa returned for a visit.

In 1858 William and Jennie McGaa were living in one of the first log cabins on the banks of Cherry Creek. At this time, McGaa and several acquaintances formed St. Charles Town and later Denver City, named after Gov. James Denver of Kansas Territory, and proceeded to sell land to the incoming pioneers. The group of men felt fortunate to have McGaa included in their plans because of his suc-

cessful dealings with the Indians and his Sioux wife. Each of the town founders was honored with a street named after him; the present Market Street in Denver once was called McGaa.

During the time the McGaas were at Cherry Creek, a historical event took place. On March 8, 1859, Jennie gave birth to their first son, the first predominantly White child born in Denver. They named him William Denver McGaa after his father and the town in which he was born. It was a very exciting day and was looked upon as a stroke of good luck for the community. The McGaas had two other children, John, who died at age 4, and Jessie.

In the spring of 1861, the family moved north to the town of Colona, or Laporte as it is now called, in the Cache La Poudre Valley. Their lives remained fairly stable until August 1864, when Indian troubles broke out in full force. No one knows whether William McGaa went to war or back to England to visit his parents, but between 1864 and 1867 he left his family in Laporte and never returned.

After several years of waiting, Jennie began to believe he had been killed. She married Joseph Brown, another Denver pioneer. They remained in Laporte, and had three children: Joseph Jr., George R. and Jennie.

Mrs. Hazel McGaa Cuney, Denver McGaa's daughter, recalls that one day William McGaa, whom they thought was dead, showed up at their cabin in Laporte. When he found he had lost his family, he was heartbroken and returned to Denver. Though not a drinking man, he found comfort in liquor. On Dec. 15, 1867, while in Denver, he was put in jail to sober up. The old building was not well ventilated and McGaa, at age 45, died in it during the night. He is buried in Denver.

Eleven years later, on a cold February day in 1878, Denver McGaa was summoned home by his half brother.

Deeply depressed, Jennie McGaa Brown, at 35, was dying from poison she had taken. By the time the doctor arrived, it was too late. Other reports mention her drowning in the Poudre River, but, according to her granddaughter, she died from the poison. She is buried in one of the oldest burial grounds in northern Colorado, Bingham Hill Cemetery near Laporte.

Meanwhile, Denver, then 19, had gone to live with his grandmother. For two years he worked as a cowboy in Colorado and Wyoming, and in 1880 he left Laporte with his grandmother and returned to his mother's people at Pine Ridge Indian Reservation in South Dakota. For the next 12 years, he worked in government service at Pine Ridge, serving as Indian census-taker, herdsman, scout, guide and interpreter.

In 1892 he was given the position of assistant farmer and he taught the Sioux to farm and manage cattle. In 1894 he became the Indian trader at Pine Ridge and had a very admirable record. Later, he became a very prosperous stock rancher in Pennington County, South Dakota, owning more than 1,000 head of cattle and a large herd of fine-bred horses.

Denver McGaa often bought his cattle in Denver and drove them back to South Dakota himself. He had a deep respect for the town in which he was born. He fathered 13 children, surviving several of them plus two wives. His oldest son was named after him, as he was proud of the name "Denver." His third wife, Mary Pourier McGaa, is still alive (she is 96). William Denver McGaa died in 1925 at the age of 66; he is buried on the Pine Ridge Reservation. ∎

In this newspaper article written by Susan Hall, William McGaa is portrayed as a man who did not drink and turned to alcohol to ease his broken heart. After reading more than a half dozen accounts to the contrary from various Denver area settlers with narratives describing McGaa as "shifty," "a troublesome customer to manage," and "William McGaa, a mountain man of questionable reputation who was disliked by his peers," I postulate that the McGaa family wished to clean up his tarnished reputation when being interviewed by Hall.

The following is from the writings of E.P. Stout, who arrived at the South Platte shortly after the Lawrence Party. Stout was a stockholder and President of the Denver City Town Company, 1859, and a delegate from Denver City to the first Constitutional Convention on June 11.

"Our party, consisting of myself and two others, with a four-horse team, left Omaha on the 26th day of September 1858, and arrived at the mouth of Cherry Creek on the 26th day of October. We were met by "Jack Jones" and John Smith, traders with the Cheyenne and Arapaho Indians, who were living on the site of Denver. That evening these two traders invited us to visit them and feast with them. We did so and were treated to a good meal by Jones' squaw wife. It wound up with a hot whiskey stew made from whiskey distilled from wheat and called "Taos Lightning." From the effect it produced on Jones and Smith, one would readily have concluded that it was genuine fighting whiskey. When it began to take effect those two gentlemen seemed to be seized with a fiendish desire to slaughter one another, and with their Colt revolvers commenced a rapid fusillade upon each other. As that kind of entertainment was rather too vigorous for us "tenderfeet," we managed to slide out through the darkness, making our way to our own tents, leaving our hosts to the tender mercies of each other, and expecting to find next morning both of them riddled with bullets."

Before Market Street in downtown Denver was named Market Street, it was called Holladay Street; before that, it was McGaa Street. As one of the first streets platted in Denver, it was indeed named after William McGaa, but McGaa had participated in too many unscrupulous business deals in the Denver region, and the accolade of having a street named after him was short-lived.

"Unsurprisingly, McGaa was a not-great representative of the newly birthed city on the plains. He was prone to violence, and the ready supply of strong liquor in Denver fueled his bad behavior. By 1866 he had burned all his bridges, and the City gave McGaa Street a new name, Holladay Street." ~ Denver Public Library.

Whatever his faults may have been, McGaa was a persuasive, enterprising individual whom no one ever forgot once they had met him, and he was definitely one of the founders of Denver. His exploits, of which there were many, have been documented in history. He is one of the larger-than-life characters from the Wild West who continues to immortalize the image of the decadent, daring frontiersman.

This 1850s sketch was identified as William McGaa and was supposedly drawn from a tintype photograph.

LaRocque headstone before reconstruction

LaRocque headstone after reconstruction

Jennie's stepfather, Alphonse LaRocque, passed away on November 18, 1877, three months before Jennie, and she was buried near his gravesite in Bingham Hill Cemetery. Alphonse LaRocque had been issued a patent for 160 acres in Larimer County in 1870. The land was located on township 8 north, range 69 west. After his death, his land was almost immediately transferred to Peter Duhamel on December 5, 1877. I do not know if Aŋpaha received anything for this prime property as there is no recorded Transfer of Deed in her name. However, women were not allowed to own land in 1877, especially a Native woman. If Duhamel was a trusted friend of Alphonse, he may have used his own name on the paperwork to give the money to Aŋpaha. In the book, "History of the Bingham Hill Cemetery, LaPorte & Bellvue, Colorado," Brinks wrote, "After he [LaRocque] died, his Indian wife, Mary, sold the land to Tobias Miller. John Lyon, guardian for LaRocque's minor daughter, Louisa, sued and 70 acres was returned to Louisa, the rest going to Miller, and later to the Michauds."

I researched Larimer County records regarding Brink's statement and could not find any documents that showed Aŋpaha (Mary) was involved in any land transaction. The Larimer County Clerk & Recorder sent me all the documents they had on file pertaining to LaRocque and his land. She responded, "There are only 5 documents between 1872-1886 that contain the name Alphonse LaRocque. I cannot find anything with Mary's name." All the documents she sent me had the names of Alphonse LaRocque and Peter Duhamel. I am unsure where Brinks got her information about Tobias Miller and the Michauds, but I do hope that Aŋpaha received her money for the sale of their land.

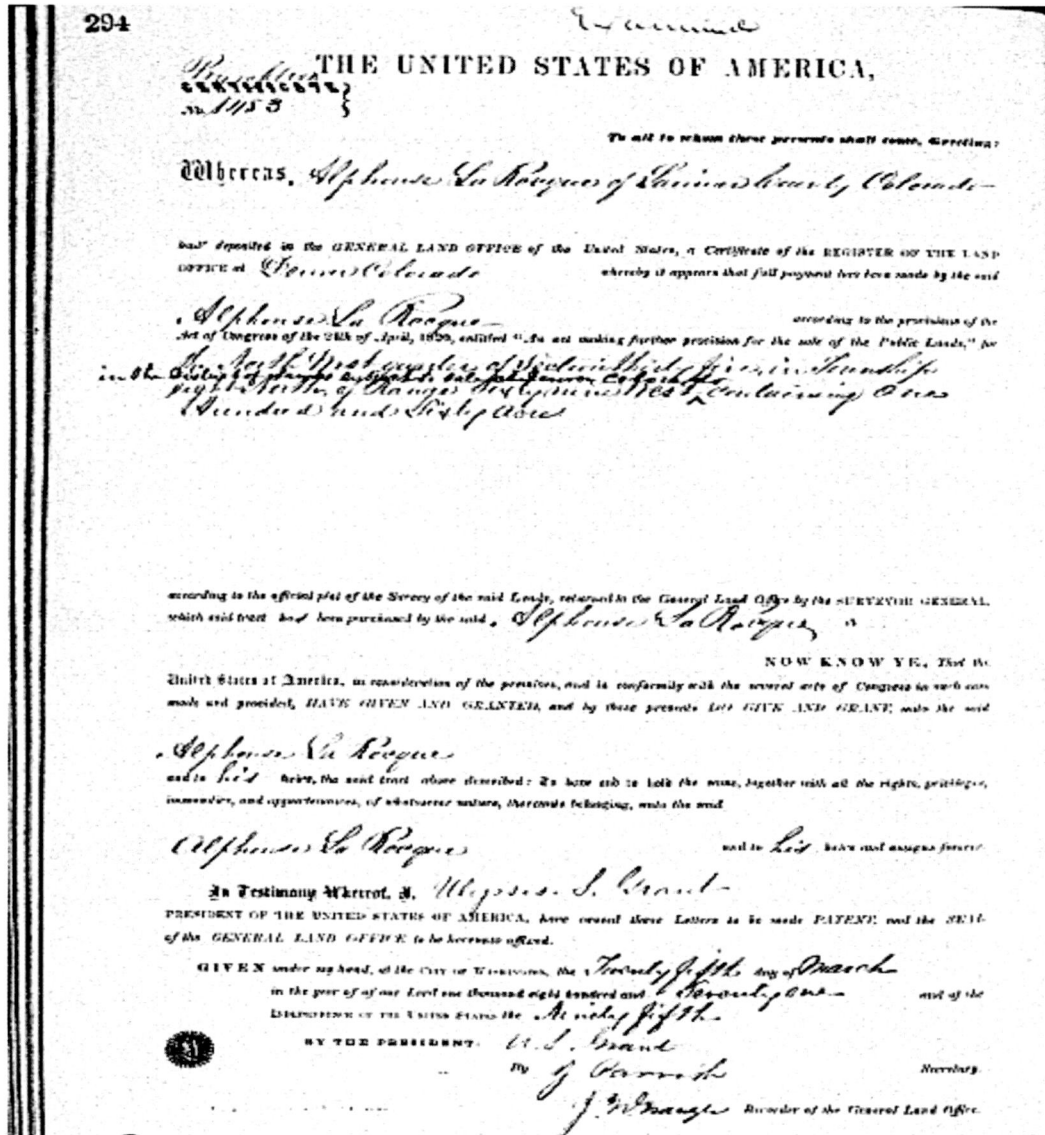

The land patent that was issued to LaRocque in 1870.

No. 5312.

Know all men by these presents,

That I, Peter Duhamel of the County of Weld and State of Colorado for and in consideration of one Dollar to me in hand paid and for other good and valuable considerations, the receipt whereof is hereby confessed do hereby grant, bargain, sell, convey, release and quitclaim unto Alphonse La Rogue of the County of Larimer and State of ____ the right title interest claim or demand whatsoever I may have acquired in through or by a certain Indenture or Mortgage Deed, bearing date the sixteenth (16) day of December AD 1871 and recorded in the recorder's office of Larimer County and State of Colorado in Book I of records page 276 & 277 to the premises therein described to wit: — The north west quarter of section thirty five (35) in Township Eight (8) North of range sixty nine (69) West.

And which said Mortgage Deed was made to secure one certain promissory note bearing even date with said deed for the sum of Five hundred ($500) Dollars and cents.

Witness my hand and seal this fifth (5) day of December AD 1877

Peter Duhamel. [seal]

State of Colorado }
Larimer County } ss   I, Chas P. Bell County Clerk in and for said County in the State aforesaid do hereby certify that Peter Duhamel personally known to me as the same person whose name is subscribed to the foregoing deed appeared before me this day in person, and acknowledged that he signed sealed and delivered the said instrument of writing as his free and voluntary act for the uses and purposes therein set forth.

Given under my hand and seal this fifth (5) day of December AD 1877

Chas P. Bell
County Clerk

Filed for record at 11 o'clock A.m. 5th Dec AD 1877

$500 Mortgage Deed secured by Duhamel in the County of Larimer. Dated December 1877.

Joseph Brown is on the left, and his stepson, William Denver McGaa, is on the right. The older girl standing beside Joseph is his stepdaughter and Denver's younger sister, Jessie McGaa, daughter of William and Jennie. The girl with her arm on Denver's chair is Louise LaRocque, daughter of Aŋpaha and Alphonse LaRocque and Jennie's half-sister. The girl sitting down is Jennie Brown Jr., Joseph and Jennie's daughter. The three girls' identities are not documented on the back of the picture, but their apparent ages make me confident that this is correct. Joseph would have been 39, Denver 20, Jessie 18, Louise 12, and Jennie 5. This looks like it may have been taken at Jennie's funeral.

After Jennie's unexpected death, Joseph was left with three small children: Joseph Jr. was nine, George was seven, and Jennie Jr. was five. Denver came to help for a brief time, but he was 20 years old and thinking about starting his own family. I assume that Aŋpaha helped care for Little Jennie for a while, but she had lost both her husband and daughter within three months and, deep in mourning, was relying on Joseph for protection and food.

Xenophobia was emerging in the Cache la Poudre Valley. The white settlers in La Porte had been busy organizing it into a "civilized" town, and their animosity towards the Native wives was intensifying to an alarming level. The French-Indian families had established the town to escape the rising racism in Denver, but it was now apparent that colonization and racial intolerance had appeared in their prosperous little community. Newspaper coverage written by white journalists fueled the hatred by falsely accusing the local Natives of supporting their "wild and hostile relatives." The press described them as "savage heathens and bloodthirsty animals" who needed to be removed from white territory. The U.S. government dispatched a cavalry regiment to Colorado to do just that.

The majority of the French husbands left the area with their Native wives to start over on the Pine Ridge Reservation in South Dakota. This was the final forced exodus of white men, Indian wives, and their mixed-blood progeny from the Colorado area. Aŋpaha had been living in the Jefferson Territory for over 20 years. She witnessed the emergence of the city of Denver and underwent the ensuing relocation from Cherry Creek to Cache la Poudre, where she and Alphonse worked hard to acquire land and build a life. Now, she was being pushed out again.

She and her daughter, Louise, returned to the Oglala people in South Dakota, traveling with other Lakotans living in the Poudre Valley. Louise married Charles Cuny Sr. in Pine Ridge, and Aŋpaha lived out her final days in their home near Cuny Table in the Badlands. Aŋpaha died in 1905 and is buried in the Red Cloud Cemetery in Pine Ridge, South Dakota.

Louise LaRocque Cuny with her daughter

Joseph did not want to stay in LaPorte with his memories of Jennie, especially since his friends had left for the Pine Ridge Reservation. He moved to the remote area of Horseshoe Gulch, South Park, CO., trying his luck at mining once again before investing in a team of oxen that could traverse the steep mountain roads. With his two sons as his companions, he expanded his freighting business. Their main route was the central line from Denver to Horseshoe Gulch and then to Leadville. This circuit was probably the most treacherous and challenging trail in the state. At 10,152 feet above sea level, Leadville is North America's highest elevated incorporated city. I recently visited the historic town. I cannot imagine maneuvering a heavily loaded freight wagon powered by a team of oxen, plodding up a rugged mountain trail, and then descending the mountain's switchbacks to Denver. Joseph Brown had to have been made of true grit and fortitude.

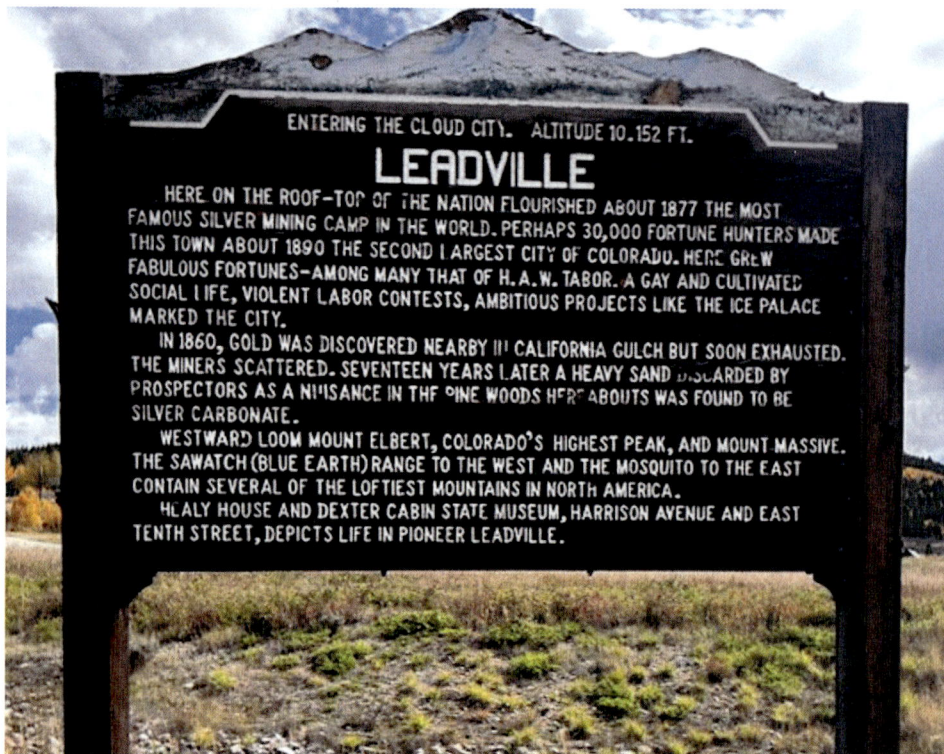

Leadville photo by Tracy Hauff, 2022

The 1880 Census for Horseshoe Gulch, Park County, Colorado, lists Joseph Brown, Miner, age 42; Joseph Brown, Son, age 11; and George Brown, Son, age 9. There is no mention of Little Jennie in Joseph's household, but the 1880 Census for Fairplay, Park County, Colorado, shows that William and Catherine Southland adopted Jennie, and she was a member of their household. Joseph probably did what he felt was best for Jennie. Park County was a wild mining district inhabited by unsavory characters and was certainly no place for a little girl without a mother. Joseph continued his relationship with Jennie, and she was living with him in Shannon County in 1897 when she married David Robinson. She went by the last name of Brown until she married.

As much as Horseshoe Gulch was no place for a little girl, it was also unsuitable for a young boy. George Brown disappears from all records around the age of twelve or thirteen. By Sylvan's account, he went to Carlisle Indian School in Pennsylvania, but Superintendent Henry Pratt at Carlisle kept exceptional documents and records of the students, and there is no documentation of George Brown enrolling or attending the school. I thought another possibility might be the United States Indian Industrial Trading School, known as Haskell, which opened in 1884 in Kansas and was also actively recruiting Indian children. George would have been 13 years old in 1884. I contacted the Archives Specialist at the National Archives in Kansas City to ask him to run a record check on both Haskell and Genoa Indian Boarding School in Nebraska. His search included the Department of the Interior and the Office of Indian Affairs at Pine Ridge Agency, Rosebud Agency, and Cheyenne River Agency. A name match for George Racine Brown was not found.

The State Industrial School for Boys was established in Golden, Colorado in 1881. This reform school operated as a trade school for boys ages 7 – 16. Is it possible that George could have ended up here? A teenage boy who lost his mother when he was young and had to work physical labor for his father might have become rebellious. I will continue my search, but for now, we know that when George returned home six years later, he had been trained in the trades of blacksmithing, harness-making, and farming—skills taught at a trade school. He could read and write and clearly understood math and business.

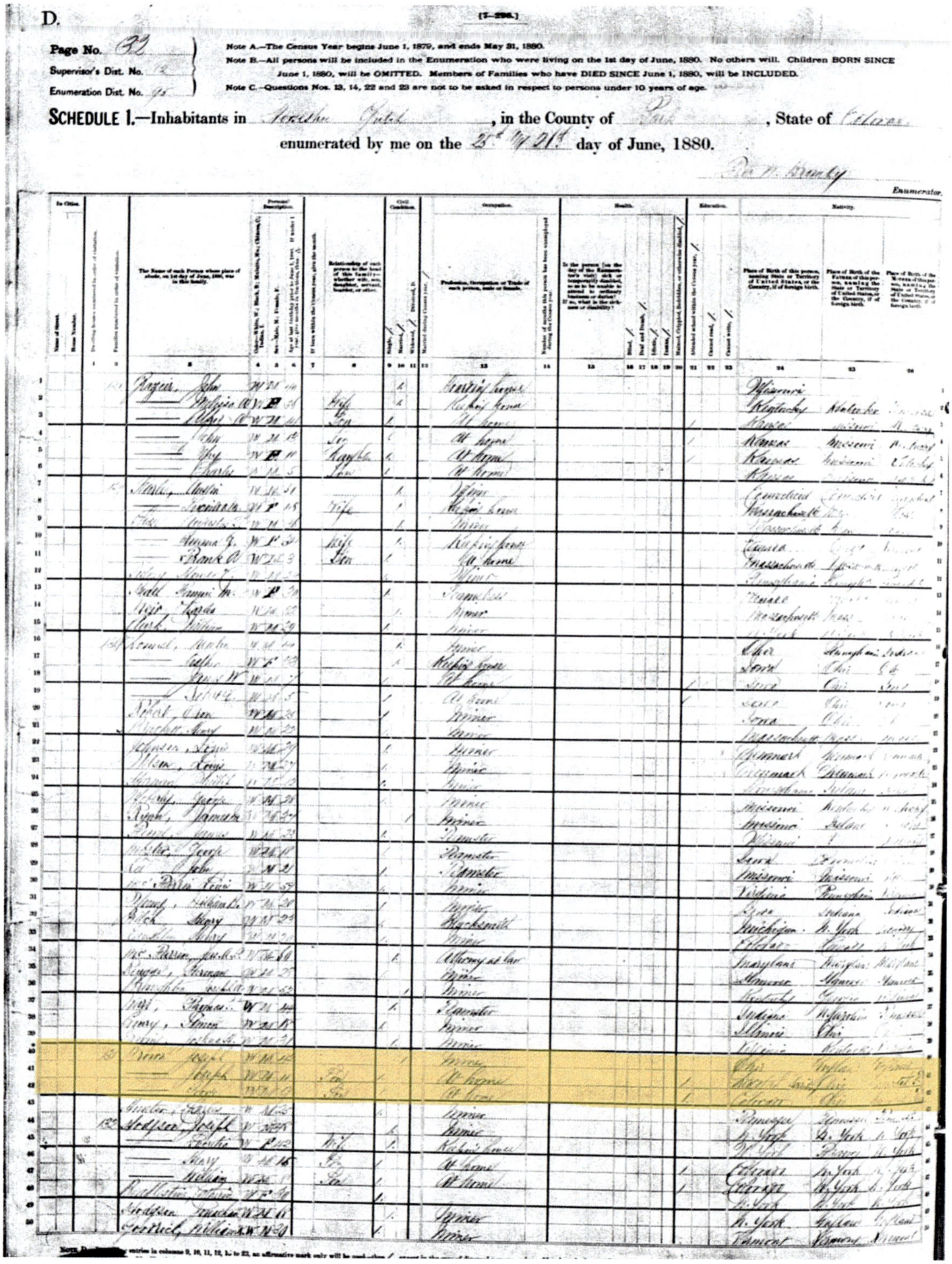

Page No. 32

Supervisor's Dist. No.

Enumeration Dist. No. 95

[7—296.]

Note A.—The Census Year begins June 1, 1879, and ends May 31, 1880.

Note B.—All persons will be included in the Enumeration who were living on the 1st day of June, 1880. No others will. Children BORN SINCE June 1, 1880, will be OMITTED. Members of Families who have DIED SINCE June 1, 1880, will be INCLUDED.

Note C.—Questions Nos. 13, 14, 22 and 23 are not to be asked in respect to persons under 10 years of age.

SCHEDULE 1.—Inhabitants in _Horseshoe Gulch_, in the County of _Park_, State of _Colorado_,

enumerated by me on the _28 & 29_ day of June, 1880.

Geo. W. Brumly Enumerator.

1880 Census, Horseshoe Gulch, Park County, Colorado, listing Joseph, Joseph Jr., and George Brown.

1880 Census, Fairplay, Park County, Colorado. Jennie Brown, age 7, is the sixth row from the bottom.

Joseph and Elizabeth (Jackson) Rooks c. 1810 – 1820.

The Rook's ancestry traces back to England and Ireland. Joseph Rooks, born in Kentucky in 1772, was married to Elizabeth Jackson. Their son, John Rooks, was born in Ohio in 1808 and married Temperance Jackson. John and Temperance had six children together. Joseph Oliver Rooks, their fourth child, was born in 1846 in Putnam County, Missouri. He was 15 years old when the Civil War broke out in 1861, and eager to enlist, he ran away from home to join Company M of the 7th Missouri Cavalry, Union Army. He was honorably discharged in Little Rock, Arkansas, on February 29, 1864, but immediately reenlisted to join Company I of the 1st Missouri Cavalry, where he became a Corporal. His personal description at the time of enlistment was 5 feet, 10 inches, light complexion with blue eyes, and auburn hair.

5—889

DEPARTMENT OF THE INTERIOR
BUREAU OF PENSIONS

WASHINGTON, D. C., January 2, 1915.

SIR: Please answer, at your earliest convenience, the questions enumerated below. The information is requested for future use, and it may be of great value to your widow or children. Use the inclosed envelope, which requires no stamp.

Very respectfully,

JOSEPH ROOKS,   KADOKA, S. DAK.
1165372

U. S. APR 16 1915 PENSION OFFICE

No. 1. Date and place of birth? *Answer.* On the 16th day of March 1846 at Unionville, Putnam County, Missouri.
The name of organizations in which you served? *Answer.* Co. M. 7th Mo. Cav. & Co. I. 1st. Mo. Cav. was a corporal in Co. I. 1st. Mo. Cav.

No. 2. What was your post office at enlistment? *Answer.* Unionville, Missouri.

No. 3. State your wife's full name and her maiden name. *Answer.* Kate Rooks formerly Kate Robinson

No. 4. When, where, and by whom were you married? *Answer.* Married Feb. 22nd. 1873 at the Old Spotted Tail Agency near Fort Robinson, Neb. By Act-Agent Robert Cox. The next summer they were re-married by the Rev. Hinman at the Mount
No. 5. Is there any official or church record of your marriage? of Ash Creek near the Spotted Tail Agenc
If so, where? *Answer.* So far as I know there is no church or official record of the marri

No. 6. Were you previously married? If so, state the name of your former wife, the date of the marriage, and the date and place of her death or divorce. If there was more than one previous marriage, let your answer include all former wives. *Answer.*
I was married in Colorado 26 miles South of Cheyenne, Wyo. in December 1866 to Tingaliska a full blood Sioux woman she died in April 1872 at Mouth of Ash Creek near Ft. Robinson.
No other former marriage

No. 7. If your present wife was married before her marriage to you, state the name of her former husband, the date of such marriage, and the date and place of his death or divorce, and state whether he ever rendered any military or naval service, and, if so, give name of the organization in which he served. If she was married more than once before her marriage to you, let your answer include all former husbands. *Answer.* Kate Rooks was never married before.

No. 8. Are you now living with your wife, or has there been a separation? *Answer.* I am now and ever since our marriage have lived with my wife Kate Rooks.

In August 1866, President Lincoln declared an end to the Civil War that had claimed the lives of over 600,000 American men. Joseph headed west in the company of other adventurous young survivors, settling first in present-day Colorado along Box Elder Creek, a small stream that begins 25 miles southwest of Cheyenne, Wyoming, and empties into the Cache La Poudre River. He found employment with E. W. Whitcomb as an overland freighter hauling potatoes and wood between Fort Collins and Fort Laramie. With the advent of the Union Pacific

Railroad, Cheyenne would be added to his route the following year when it debuted as a notorious railroad town with pugnacious inhabitants.

In December 1866, on the Whitcomb ranch situated where the Cache La Poudre River meets Box Elder Creek, Joseph met a young, full-blooded Lakota woman, Tiṅgleška, who was living there with her half-sister, Emilie Chatillon Lessert. Whitcomb was married to an Oglala Lakota woman—Katherine (Kate Shaw) Whitcomb—and his ranch was well-known for welcoming white traders, their Native wives, and any of his wife's Native relatives. The Whitcombs took in Kate's nephew—eight-year-old Baptiste (Little Bat) Garnier—after his Lakota mother died. Baptiste's father had been killed by the Cheyenne Indians in 1856. Little Bat lived with the Whitcombs until he was eighteen. He became one of the Cavalry's most trusted scouts and interpreters. He was well-liked by the Lakota people and the U.S. Army. Little Bat was murdered in cold blood in Crawford, Nebraska, in 1900. There is a plaque on the corner of Main Street and 2nd Street in Crawford in remembrance of the government scout.

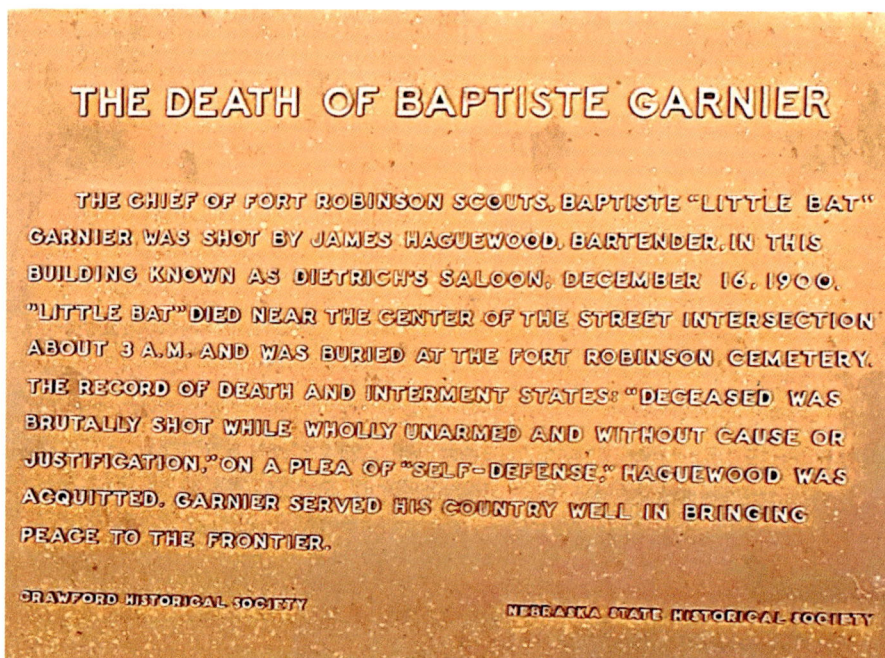

THE DEATH OF BAPTISTE GARNIER

THE CHIEF OF FORT ROBINSON SCOUTS, BAPTISTE "LITTLE BAT" GARNIER WAS SHOT BY JAMES HAGUEWOOD, BARTENDER, IN THIS BUILDING KNOWN AS DIETRICH'S SALOON, DECEMBER 16, 1900. "LITTLE BAT" DIED NEAR THE CENTER OF THE STREET INTERSECTION ABOUT 3 A.M. AND WAS BURIED AT THE FORT ROBINSON CEMETERY. THE RECORD OF DEATH AND INTERMENT STATES: "DECEASED WAS BRUTALLY SHOT WHILE WHOLLY UNARMED AND WITHOUT CAUSE OR JUSTIFICATION." ON A PLEA OF "SELF-DEFENSE," HAGUEWOOD WAS ACQUITTED. GARNIER SERVED HIS COUNTRY WELL IN BRINGING PEACE TO THE FRONTIER.

CRAWFORD HISTORICAL SOCIETY   NEBRASKA STATE HISTORICAL SOCIETY

Photo by Tracy Hauff, 2024.

The plaque reads:

The Death of Baptiste Garnier

The Chief of Fort Robinson Scouts, Baptiste "Little Bat" Garnier was shot by James Haguewood, Bartender in this building known as Dietrich's Saloon, December 16, 1900. Little Bat died near the center of the street intersection about 3 A.M. and was buried at the Fort Robinson Cemetery. The record of death and internment states "Deceased was brutally shot while wholly unarmed and without cause or justification." On a plea of "self-defense" Haguewood was acquitted. Garnier served his country well in bringing peace to the Frontier.

Baptiste "Little Bat" Garnier

E.W. Whitcomb and grandchildren. The small photo is of his wife, Katherine Shaw Whitcomb.
Photo courtesy of the Fort Collins Museum of Discovery.
Photo of Kate is courtesy of Wyoming State Archives.

E.W. Whitcomb was a vibrant, renowned figure in the Fort Collins/Cheyenne/Fort Laramie area. He could be rough and stern while also gentle and compassionate. It is believed his gentlemanly conduct kept him from the history pages of infamy. He brought the first Longhorn cattle from Texas to the Wyoming territory and was responsible for hiring gunmen to kill cattle rustlers, which eventually became a widespread problem that escalated into the Johnson County War. He said he did this "because I can't abide thieves." He hired the legendary gunfighter Tom Horn, who named his favorite horse E.W., in honor of Whitcomb. Some say that Robert LeRoy Parker and Harry Longabaugh, better known as Butch Cassidy and the Sundance Kid, worked briefly for Whitcomb before they became illustrious train robbers. Lakota and Arapaho warriors raided Whitcomb's ranch regularly, stealing his cattle and horses, but Whitcomb was tolerant of these actions, deciding it came with the territory. It was the dishonest actions of white men that he couldn't tolerate. I bet he regretted ever hiring Butch Cassidy and the Sundance Kid.

Tiŋgléška and Emilie were Bear Robe's daughters, Chief Bull Bear's granddaughters, and Little Wound's nieces. Tiŋgléška's father was a full-blood Lakota man, and Emilie's father was French fur trader Henri Chatillon. Bear Robe was the daughter of Chief Bull Bear, the imposing Oglala leader killed in 1841 by Red Cloud. Smoke, a leader of the Bad Face band, raised Red Cloud after his parents died. The feud between Bull Bear and Smoke started months earlier when someone told Bull Bear that Smoke wanted to be the headman of the Kuhinyan band in addition to his own Bad Face band. Upon hearing this, Bull Bear issued a challenge against Smoke by killing Smoke's favorite horse. This was a grave insult that could not be ignored, and Red Cloud retaliated. Fur traders were in the camp that night on Chugwater Creek, and liquor was involved in the climactic fight. Bull Bear's death at the hands of Red Cloud separated the Oglala into two factions. The Bear People broke camp immediately after the fight, renaming their band Kiyuksa, meaning "break in two, cut in the middle."

Bull Bear had been friendly with the white traders and frequented the trading posts. Under his son's leadership, Bull Bear's band remained along the Platte and Republican Rivers in southwestern Nebraska and the upper northeast corner of Colorado, becoming allies with the Southern Cheyenne. Smoke went north to the Powder River Country. The Bear People went to live with the Southern Oglalas, while Smoke joined the groups of Northern Oglalas.

David Adams, a fur trader in partnership with John Sibille, wrote about the killing of Bull Bear in his journal: "the 24 friday Dec 1841 Mr. Shatran [Chartran] men got in the vilag this evning and brot with him 2 cags of milk [2 kegs of whiskey] and he began to trad and he did mak a bit of a trad he traded out 5 galons of milk [whiskey] and got 9 robs and wasant that a splendid trad we got the news of bool bear and 7 outher bravs death thay ar all ogalas and thay fot between them selvs and split ther vilig. it was all on a count of jelosy."

Adams was a phonetic speller, and his journal becomes easier to read once you recognize that he didn't use capitalization and never put an 'e' at the end of any word. Punctuation is almost non-existent. He cleverly referred to whiskey as milk.

My maternal great-great-grandfather, Hubert Rouleau, a French-Canadian fur trapper, witnessed the killing of Bull Bear. In his iconic book, The Oregon Trail, Francis Parkman, historian and author, wrote, "Rouleau was present and told me the particulars. The tumult became general, and was not quelled until several had fallen on both sides. When we were in the country the feud between the two families was still rankling."

David Adams' journal backs up Rouleau's claim. Adams wrote about several encounters with Rouleau in 1841-1845 along the fur trading routes. "Mr. Rulow [Rouleau] past hear to day he has moved in with all of his aquipment he had a small wagon it was loded with his goods and a lady and a few robs."

Bull Bear the Older, the headman of the Kuhinyan. Painting by Alfred Jacob Miller.

Bear Robe's husband, Henri Chatillon, was employed by Francis Parkman in 1846 when she died. The friendship between the two men began in St. Louis, where Parkman was looking for a guide for his trip west. Parkman was struck by Chatillon's gentle, kind spirit that seemed curiously incongruent with the tales of his courage and confident dealings with the Plains Indians. Another favorable aspect was that Chatillon's wife, Bear Robe, was the daughter of the high-ranking Oglala Lakota leader, Bull Bear. Parkman knew Chatillon was the man he wanted as his principal escort for his excursion into the west to observe the Titonwan in Nebraska Territory.

It was well-known that Chatillon loved his Lakota wife and was profoundly distraught by her passing. Everyone around him felt his grief, and Parkman wrote about Bear Robe's death in detail, of which I have excerpted the following:

"The squaw of Henry Chatillon, a woman with whom he had been connected for years by the strongest ties which in that country exist between the sexes, was dangerously ill. She and her children were in the village of The Whirlwind, at the distance of a few days' journey. Henry was anxious to see the woman before she died, and provide for the safety and support of his children, of whom he was extremely fond. To have refused him this would have been inhumanity… And where was Henry's squaw?—coming as fast as she could, with Mahto-Tatonka [Bull Bear the Younger] and the rest of her brothers, but she would never reach us, for she was dying, and asking every moment for Henry. Henry's manly face became clouded and downcast." [Henri rode with little rest until he found the lodges of his wife and her brothers, who were traveling on their way to meet him. They were in a dangerous situation as enemy Crow warriors were stalking them.] "The woman lay in one of them [lodges], reduced to a mere skeleton. For some time she had been unable to move or speak. Indeed, nothing had kept her alive but the hope of seeing Henry, to whom she was strongly and faithfully attached. No sooner did he enter the lodge than she revived, and she talked with him the greater part of the night. Early in the morning, she was lifted into a travois, and the whole party set out towards our camp. Henry was riding with Shaw when Mahto-Tatonka, a younger brother of the woman, hastily called after them. Turning back, they found all the Indians crowded around the travois in which the woman was lying. They reached her just in time to hear the death rattle in her throat. In a moment she lay dead. A complete stillness succeeded; then the Indians raised in concert their cries of lamentation over the corpse…Henry left her to the care of her relatives and came immediately with Shaw to the camp. It was some time before he entirely recovered from his dejection."

Henri returned to his family in St. Louis, Tiŋgleška was with the Kiyuksa Bear People, and Emilie was taken to the home of Joseph Bissonette, a fellow fur trader and long-time friend of Henri's. She was raised as part of the Bissonette family, but Henri made regular visits from St. Louis to see her, and they stayed connected for the remainder of his life. Emilie had no desire to live in St. Louis, although she and her husband Ben were married there on January 3, 1859, in the Catholic Church as was Henri's wish. Emilie was baptized in Carondelet a few days before the marriage ceremony. This was also at Henri's request.

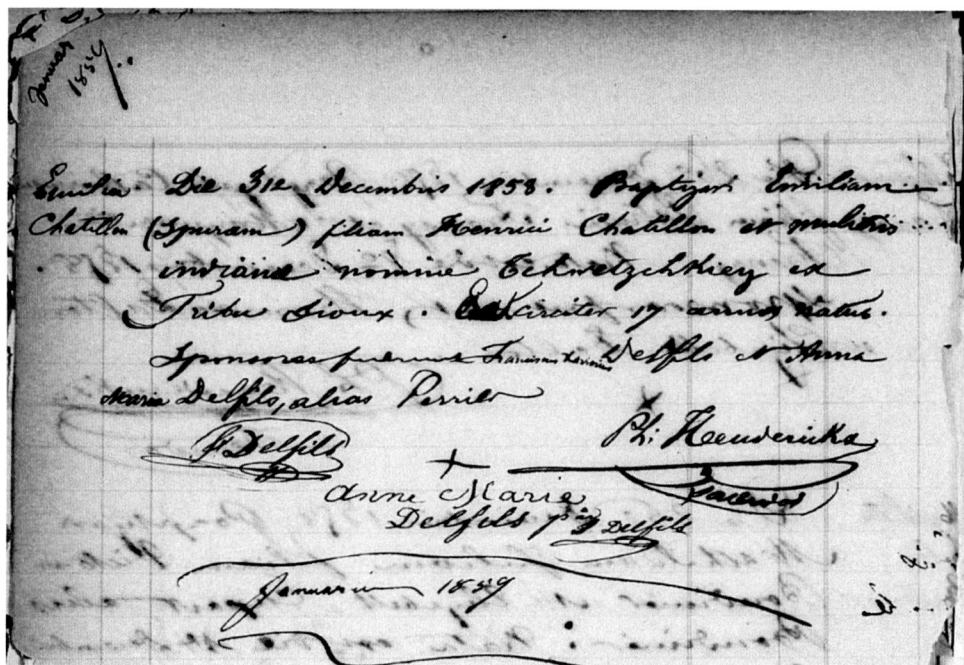

Emilie Chatillon Baptismal Record, December 31, 1858.
Saints Mary and Joseph Catholic Church Records 1821-1993

Henri Chatillon

Emilie Chatillon Lessert

Residing back in St. Louis, Henri built a four-room house that was eventually transformed into a historic mansion. He remarried in 1848 to Odile Delor Lux, and they moved into the new house. Sometime between 1847 and 1856, he commissioned an artist to create a painting in the likeness of Bear Robe, which is now hanging in the historic Chatillon-DeMenil Mansion in St. Louis. The picture is intriguing; it is an afterlife depiction with two representations of Bear Robe, one of a younger woman and one of her age at the time of her death. In the background is a bear robe, and along the bottom across her chest is the white horse she rode that was killed and buried with her. Henri Chatillon is in the lower left corner, and her horse is running across a mountain landscape in the lower right—perhaps a fond memory of how Chatillon wanted to remember them as a couple.

The mansion was purchased by the Landmarks Association in 1964, and a historical renovation began. The painting was discovered hidden in the attic rafters, wrapped around a Hawken rifle (a gift from Francis Parkman), and covered with leather. It had been hidden for over one hundred years. Did Henri put it there so Odile would not find it? Did Odile insist that he get rid of it? Did one of their descendants try to hide Henri's first love? It could be any of these, and along with Parkman's account, it is yet another testament to Henri's love for his Lakota wife.

Henri Chatillon commissioned this painting of Bear Robe. Artist unknown.

Bull Bear's second son, Little Wound, accepted the responsibility of caring for Tiŋgleška after Bear Robe died in 1846. Twenty years later, he, or another member of the Bear People, escorted her to the Whitcomb ranch for her safety when the turbulent Red Cloud Wars began in 1866. Red Cloud, Crazy Horse, and Hump led these wars to defend the last treasured hunting grounds of the Lakota—the Powder River country in Wyoming. In 1868, Whitcomb took his children to LaPorte to get them away from the Red Cloud Wars, which now involved relentless raiding of the settlers' ranches in addition to burning down the forts. Rooks and Tiŋgleška had been in LaPorte but were now at Fort Laramie.

When Rooks met Tiŋgleška in 1866, Little Wound was the leader of the Kiyuksa. Bull Bear the Younger had been killed the previous year in a fight with the Shoshone, and with Little Wound's intellect, diplomacy, and courage, he was the logical choice to lead. Rooks knew he wanted Little Wound's niece, Tiŋgleška, to be his wife and offered the Bull Bear family a horse in exchange for the right to marry her, in harmony with the Lakota custom.

Little Wound with his son, George, and his wife. c. 1899

Little Wound, seated 2nd from the right. Photo by C.M. Bell, 1877

Two years later, Rooks and Tiŋgléška were married in a legal ceremony by the Justice of the Peace. As previously mentioned, it was a double ceremony with Joseph and Jennie Brown held at the home of Ben and Emilie Lessert (Claymore) in Larimer County on August 10, 1868. The marriage certificate was issued to "Joseph Rooks and Ann Claymore." Joseph and Tiŋgléška agreed that she would go by this name for her protection. The white settlers at this time strongly disapproved of the marriages between white men and native women, even though this had been perfectly acceptable in the western territories before the influx of pioneer families. The newly arrived white women were particularly hostile toward the native wives, resenting their adaptation to white culture and dress. Joseph was a religious man, and I believe the formal ceremony was important to him, too. In addition to pressure from the settlers, the federal government had sent orders for the military to move the Natives out of areas populated by whites, especially those near the route of the Union Pacific Railroad.

Rooks and Tiŋgléška did not stay long in the Cache la Poudre region, relocating to Fort Laramie, where the population of Lakota had been steadily increasing since 1865; approximately two thousand were now camped around the North Platte and Laramie Rivers. Joseph Rooks Jr. was born here during the signing of the 1868 Fort Laramie Treaty. The government had been complaining about having to feed the large numbers of Indians at Fort Laramie and had already made up their minds that they should be moved to an agency. This was made clear with Article 4 of the freshly signed treaty: "The United States agrees at its own proper expense, to construct at some place on the Missouri River, near the center of said reservation…" The military wasted no time ordering the Lakotas to pack up and begin the journey to Whetstone. They were marched by foot, horse, and wagon to the recently established Indian agency in Dakota Territory. Apprehension accompanied their every step— a gnawing fear that they would be sent to Indian Territory in Oklahoma.

The Joseph Rooks family was among a group of families called the "Squaw Band." Bordeaux and Bissonette, also "squaw men," closed their trading posts and packed up their wares to start over at the new agency with their wives and children.

"The Squaw camp at Ft. Laramie and the Loafer band were the first to be affected. Their old friends at the fort grew cold to them, and presently told them bluntly to leave. The Indians seemed bewildered and did not know what to do. The Indians and Whites from Ft. Laramie started their sorrowful march toward the Missouri in June 1868. On the thirtieth, they reached the Indian Agency at North Platte, Nebraska, and were given some supplies by Agent Patrick. Here, they were joined by 150 persons "of the same sort," and the caravan proceeded on its march to Whetstone, the new agency on the Missouri." ~ Hyde, George. Red Cloud's Folk, A History of the Oglala Sioux Indians. University of Oklahoma Press. 1937. ~

"Harney controlled and directed the removal of several western bands from Fort Laramie to Whetstone Creek. The Laramie Loafers and Squaw bands were the first groups to be removed from Fort Laramie. They were placed in government or privately contracted wagons, which moved eastward towards Whetstone Creek, Dakota Territory, in June 1868.

During August 1868, the Laramie Loafers, Squaw bands, and their traders arrived in Dakota Territory. They set up camp nearly thirty miles north of Fort Randall on the west bank of the Missouri River, north of the mouth of Whetstone Creek." ~ Clow, Richmond L. The Whetstone Indian Agency. 1868-1872. SD State Historical Society. 1977. ~

The Fort Laramie Lakota (Loafers Around the Fort) were western Plains Indians, predominantly Oglala and Sičangu, who did not want to move to the Missouri River. They were well aware of the hordes of mosquitos, infertile soil, and lack of game in the area that was to be their new destination. They knew buffalo hunters had decimated the mighty Tatanka. If they could not live along their beloved Platte River, they preferred to live in the Powder River, Tongue River, and Black Hills areas, where elk and deer were still plentiful. The government's sole objective was to remove the Lakota from the entire Platte River area to accommodate the anticipated railroad line carrying new settlers. So distasteful was the Whetstone Agency to the Sičangu that Spotted Tail set up his camp almost 50 miles from the Missouri River, and his people refused to travel to the agency to get their rations, which strangely enough were stored an additional 30 miles away at Fort Randall. Three times a month, the "squaw" men and half-breeds would make the 60-mile round trip to Fort Randall to pick up the provisions, and the agency Indians made sure that Spotted Tail's tribe received their rations. With Rooks' freighting experience and his previous employment with Whitcomb, I'm sure he was one of the men chosen to pick up and deliver the rations.

It soon became clear to the men collecting the rations at Fort Randall that the Whetstone Agency was not receiving its annuities on time or in the quantity it should have. This created a short supply of rations the first winter, and as the Lakota had foreseen, game was scarce. More than one hundred children and elderly, mostly Sičangu and Wažaže people with Spotted Tail's band, perished from starvation or exposure due to the brutal winter storms.

Meanwhile, General Sheridan was not pleased with the agency's location, believing it was too close to the Missouri River where white people traveled. The Titonwans were still in the way of Western expansion. Captain Poole was sent in to evaluate the situation and discovered the lack of provisions. He also determined that the soil was not suitable for farming—again, something the Lakota already knew and tried to tell government officials before the move. Another problem related to the proximity of the Missouri River was the ease with which liquor dealers could transport their whiskey from boat to wagon to the Indians.

"In November 1869, Spotted Tail requested permission to go to Washington to speak with the president about the agency's removal. Spotted Tail and a delegation of Lakotas from Whetstone reached Washington in May 1870 and immediately Spotted Tail voiced his sentiments against the present location of Whetstone to officials in the Interior Department. He told about the liquor trade and its effect on his people and about the hardships of farming." ~ Clow, Richmond L. The Whetstone Indian Agency. 1868-1872. SD State Historical Society. 1977. ~

Susie Rooks, daughter of Joseph and Tiŋgleška, was born on March 3, 1870, at the Whetstone Indian Agency. By the Fall of 1870, the Lakota were in dire need of rations; the children and elderly continued to fall ill and die. The tribe had planted crops in the spring, but the yield that survived the drought did not amount to anything at harvest time. The Lakotas could not keep warm in the cold Dakota winter; their lodges were no longer made from warm, substantial buffalo hides but from white man's canvas and thin muslin cloth. By mid-winter, their plight became desperate, and the Department of Interior was seriously discussing relocating them, favoring a spot near the Black Hills. This was vetoed because of the proximity to the Northern Lakota tribes, who were still free-roaming under the leadership of Crazy Horse and Sitting Bull. In August 1871, a decision was made to move the Whetstone Agency Indians to the Big White Clay Creek in southwest South Dakota.

In a few months, they were forced to relocate again to the Ash Creek area northeast of Crawford, Nebraska, to the short-lived White River Whetstone Agency. Tiŋgleška gave birth here to their third child, Frank, in 1871. The birth must have been difficult because she never fully recovered her health. Joseph took her to Spotted Tail's White River agency seeking medical help. Tiŋgleška passed away there in May 1872. There are no known photographs of her.

Joseph married his second wife, Kate Robinson, at the Spotted Tail Agency along Beaver Creek a year later in 1873. This was the site of the fourth involuntary relocation for the Oglala and Sičangu tribes.

State of South Dakota
County of Stanley   ss

    Joseph Rooks, first being duly sworn, on oath deposes and
says; That in December 1866 he married an Indian woman named
Tingaliska a member of the Sioux Tribe at Mr. E. W. Whitcombs
cattle ranch on Boxelder creek about 26 miles South of Cheyenne Wyoming in what is now the state of Colorado. That they
were married according to the customs of her tribe and that
he gave her adopted mother a horse for her. That he was pre-
-sent at the Indian Councel held at Ft. Larime held in April
1868 and that he signed the treaty which was made with the
Sioux Indians at that time and place. That he lived
at the place where he was married until 1867 when he moved
about 16 miles South where he lived for one year. After the
Treaty was made at Ft. Larime he moved with his family to
the Whitestone Indian Agency where he lived until 1870 when
he moved to Ash Creek East of Ft. Robinson where he lived
until his wife died in 1872 about the last of May, she died
about 10 miles East of Ft. Robinson at the Rosebud Agency.
Of this marriage there was born to him three children as follows; Joseph Rooks, Jr.; Susie R. Rooks (now Brown); and
Frank Rooks; Joseph born in 1867, Susie born in 1869 and
Frank born in 1871. All of whom are now living.

    That on the 22 day of February 1873 he married Katharine
Robinson a mixed blood Indian woman of the Sioux Tribe a member of the Pine Ridge branch of that tribe. That he was married
this time at the Rosebud Indian Agency the ceremony being pre-
formed by the Rosebud Indian Agent, whose name was Robert Cox.
After his second marriage he lived with his wife at the mouth
of Beaver Creek about a month when he moved back to Ft. Robinson where he
lived until 1878 when he moved to the present Pine Ridge Indian Agency where he lived until 1880 when he moved to a place
on Little White River on Pine Ridge Indian Reservation about
10 miles North of Cody, Nebraska. That in 1892 he was appointed
Boss Farmer of the Pass Creek District a position which he held
until 1900. All of this time running at his ranch on Little White
River. During the time he was Boss Farmer he lived at Corn Creek
Commesary.

In 1903 he moved to his present home one mile West of Redstone Creek and about three miles South of White River. As a fruit of this second marriage there has been born to him fifteen children as follows; Alice Rooks (now Yeoman) born in 1874; Charles Rooks born in 1876; Nellie Rooks (now Bruce) born in 1878; Rosanna Rooks (now Allen) born in 1880; Nancy Rooks (now Peck) born in 1882; Martha Rooks (now Levermont) born in 1884; Delia Rooks (now Amiotte) born in 1886; William Rooks born in 1888; Christine Rooks (now $tahl) born in 1889; James Rooks born in1891; Rebecca Rooks born in 1893; Clara Rooks born in 1896; CatherineBridget Rooks born in 1898; Agnes Ruth Rooks born in1902 and Hobert Eric Rooks born in 1903. All of whom are now living. That his wife Katharine is also now living. That during all xxx the time since his first marriage in 1866 he has lived on the Rosebud and Pine Ridge Indian Reservations and that during all this time he has been engaged in the Stock business handling both cattle and horses.

Signed *Joseph Rooks*.

Subscribed and sworn to be fore me at Kadoka this 24th, day of January A.D. 1910.

F.P. Reidinger.
Notary Public within and for
Stanley County, South Dakota.

Filed in my office Jan. 26. 1910.
Charles H. Ball
Allotting Ag.

This affidavit was signed by Joseph Rooks and filed on January 26, 1910.

The Rooks lived at Ft. Robinson from 1878 – 1880 before moving to the Little White River area north of Cody, Nebraska. They had fifteen children together (four boys and eleven girls) and raised the three from his first marriage. All eighteen children lived to adulthood with large families of their own, a remarkable statistic during that time. The children in order of birth: Joseph Jr., Susie, Frank, Alice, Charles, Noresta (Nellie), Rosanna, Nancy, Martha, Delia, William (Willie), Christina, James (Jim), Rebecca (Becky), Clara, Catherine, Ruth Agnes (Aggie), and Eric (Hobart).

Joseph and Kate (Robinson) Rooks

In 1892, Joseph was hired by the Office of Indian Affairs (OIA) as a Boss Farmer. He was one of several boss farmers instructed to "take the bow and arrow out of the hands of the Indians and replace them with plow handles." Boss Farmer was a position that afforded a lot of privilege, and many men who accepted this appointment were inclined to abuse their power. In my research, I never found anything derogatory written about Joseph Rooks, but I did come across documents that exposed the dishonest dealings of unprincipled boss farmers. The majority of boss farmers were either mixed-bloods or white men married to Lakota women; the mixed-bloods were known as "Ieska," and the latter were referred to as "squaw men."

"The biggest advantage squaw men had over full bloods was that they could make business decisions without asking permission from an Indian Agent and within the capitalist system the ability to make timely and independent business decisions is not only beneficial it is necessary in order to compete." ~ Means, Jeffrey. From Buffalo to Beeves: The Transformation of the Oglala Lakota Economy, 1868-1889. University of Montana. 2001. ~

In a registered complaint sent to the Commissioner of Indian Affairs, it was stated that the squaw men on the Pine Ridge Indian Reservation had anywhere from 300 to 1,000 head of cattle, more than they were allowed. "Pass Creek District boss farmer Joseph Rooks, a white man married to an Oglala woman, reported that he owned 200 head. Boss Farmer Joseph Rooks estimated that of the 12,000 head of Oglala owned cattle in Pass Creek District, full-bloods owned between 25 to 50% though they represented by far the majority of the population." ~ Robertson, Paul. The Power of the Land: Identity, Ethnicity, and Class Among the Oglala Lakota. Routledge. 2002. ~

"Ranching was also encouraged, but most Oglalas did not have the capital to start a herd. Those successful at running steers and horses were usually children of the Ieska 'mixed-bloods,' derogatorily called "half-breeds," mainly the sons and daughters of white men who married Oglala women. These men came to the area as traders, trappers, and soldiers, the last fresh from the Civil War, seeking adventure on the Great Plains." ~ Powers, Marla N. Oglala Women: Myth, Ritual, and Reality. University of Chicago Press. 1986. ~

Joseph and Kate stayed in the Pass Creek district for approximately 10 years before moving to Red Stone Creek, the rugged section near the Badlands where the red sediment from iron seeps into the water. The name Badlands derives from the Lakota language. The translation of Mako (land) Sica (bad) is 'land that is bad.' Around 1900, Joseph resigned from his position as a boss farmer, and the Rooks became full-time ranchers. They were issued eighteen head of cattle—one bull and seventeen cows—and a team of mares. Joseph's brand, JOR, was found on the left hip of his cattle and horses. He grazed his herd on the open range in the uncultivated brush, where small watering holes were scattered throughout the basin, providing enough water to sustain them. The horses he bred were known in the region as unbreakable wild buckers. During his ranching days, it is estimated he sold between 650 to 1,000 head of cattle and 350 horses, descendants of the original livestock he received from the government. Rooks grazed his herd on the wild, barren land as most of the full-blood Lakotas did. His reputation was of a good husband and father, an honest and fair boss farmer, a hardworking rancher, and a helpful friend to all his Lakota and white neighbors. Kate was a cherished mother and friend, and the couple were deeply religious, holding church services, weddings, and baptisms at their home. When Joseph passed in 1919, he and Kate had sixty-five grandchildren and ten great-grandchildren.

Joseph Rooks is on the right.

Daughter-in-law, Annie LaPointe Rooks (left), Kate Robinson (center), daughter, Alice Rooks Yeoman (right).

Joseph and Kate Rooks with fifteen of their children.

DEATH CALLS PIONEER

Joseph Rooks Passes Away Tuesday Morning, Following A Second Stroke Of Paralysis

Tuesday morning just as the grey mists of the morning were giving way to the glorious rays of the rising sun, the Death Angel whispered "come" to the spirit of Joseph Rooks, and when the call was answered, wafted the spirit of this pioneer resident of this vicinity, to that grand and glorious Home above.

On Saturday of last week Mr. Rooks was taken with a stroke of paralysis, it being the second, and though every effort known to medical science was made it was of no avail.

Joseph Rooks was born in Missouri March 16, 1846, and when but fifteen years of age he enlisted in the United States army, serving in that organization and coming to South Dakota in 1879, and since that date has made this state his home. In 1865 Mr. Rooks was married at Cheyenne, Wyoming, and to this union was born three children. After the loss of his first wife, Mr. Rooks was again married at Fort Robinson, on February 22, 1872, and to this union were born fifteen children. Mrs. Rooks and all of the eighteen children survive to mourn the loss of a considerate and loving husband and an indulgent and kind father. Besides the wife and the children there are sixty-five grandchildren and ten great-grandchildren.

Joseph Rooks was one of the very first pioneer settlers in this country and for a number of years was an extensive cattle raiser, retiring from that business but a few years ago to take life a little more easy. Sixteen years ago he settled upon their present home place and has built up one of the nicest farm and ranch homes in this entire western country. He was a man among men, upright and honest, of a character and disposition making him lovable to every acquaintance. His wife and children were always his first thought in life and any manner in which he could make life just a trifle more pleasant for them was the road he took.

He was a God fearing man, and early in life became a member of the Presbyterian church and professed his faith in a Divine Creator, and lived the life of a Christian gentleman in every sense of the word. He was a member of Mount Moriah Lodge No. 155 of the Masonic order at this place, and also a member of Black Hills Consistory No. 3 at Deadwood, joining that organization on September 27, 1917, and he was a most firm believer of the teachings of these great orders, and when laid in his last resting place the mortal remains were adorned with the emblems of these orders.

Eleven years ago Mr. Rooks was taken with his first stroke of paralysis, and although of a hardy and rugged physical build, his life was spared only through the hardest kind of a fight, and he was left greatly weakened in strength and unable to throw off the far reaching ravages of a second attack.

His wife, Mrs. Rooks, and children, Joseph Rooks, Susie Brown, Frank Rooks, Alice Youman, Charels Rooks, Nellie Bruce, Rosanna Allen, Nancy Parks, Martha Livermont, Della Amiotte, William Rooks, Christina Stahl, James Rooks, Rebecca Livermont, Clara Smith, Catherine Rooks, Agnes Daniels and Hobert Rooks, all of whom survive and mourn the loss of a husband and father whose every thought was of their safety and comfort, find a vacant place left in their lives that even the swiftly passing years will not remove or fill, and while the tears of sorrow at the parting are coursing down their cheeks their sorrows receive the heartfelt sympathy of the hosts of friends who knew and loved and admired the upstanding character of this departed pioneer, and to them is given the consoling knowledge that Joseph Rooks so lived his life among men that he is today adding to the lights and pleasure of that Home above which we all hope to reach sooner or later, and it is the knowledge that in that Heavenly Home will be found the the spirits of such men as Joseph Rooks that makes the desire of reaching there worth living for.

The funeral services are being held this (Friday) afternoon at the ranch home south-east of Kadoka, and after a service by the Episcopal Bishop, the remains will be placed in their resting bed on the ranch, a spot picked out by Mr. Rooks prior to his death, and as the remains are lowered into the vault prepared to receive them, they will receive the honors of the Masonic order.

Joseph Rooks Obituary, The Kadoka Press, December 26, 1919

George and Susie (Rooks) Brown

While George was away at school, Joseph Brown had relocated to the Pine Ridge Indian Reservation, where he reunited with Joseph Rooks, and the good friends helped one another build their ranches. This was George's new home upon his return, and it was here that he met Susie Rooks, the daughter of Joseph and Tiŋgleška. The marriage of George and Susie in 1891 solidified the Brown/Rooks twenty-three-year friendship. They were now officially relatives (according to white man standards), and their descendants would be friends for generations to come.

Susie (Rooks) Brown

George Brown

After their wedding, George and Susie moved to Rock Springs, WY, and later to Cody on the Nebraska/South Dakota border. Around this time, George joined the Buffalo Bill Wild West Show and toured the United States for a year or two with the popular attraction, participating in the riding, roping, and fancy shooting acts. While on tour, George got terribly ill and was transported to the hospital in Gordon, Nebraska. When he recovered, he did not return to the show and moved his family to Cut Meat, where he became the proprietor of a general store. He also owned a large cattle herd, and this business flourished for ten years.

In 1906, they moved to Susie's allotted land in Red Stone Basin, northeast of Wanblee on the Pine Ridge Indian Reservation, and here they became successful ranchers. Unlike the "unbreakable wild buckers" produced by Joseph Rooks, George became known for breeding high-quality, desirable horses and became a prominent horse breeder. Dad told my sister, "He was the Rapid Chevrolet of western South Dakota."

Letter from George Brown written to his older brother, Joe, regarding the use of his stagecoach and horses. His asking price was $5 per day for the coach and $5 per day for each buckskin horse.

George's dad, Joseph Brown, died tragically on June 26, 1908, at age 72. Ever the freighter, he was hauling logs to build a new house in Red Stone Basin when he was thrown from the wagon. A back wheel ran over him, crushing his chest and killing him instantly. He is buried in the badlands on a hill southwest of the old Brown home.

Joseph Brown, aged 72 years, who lives with his son George Brown, near Big Cedar Bluff in Redstone Basin about fifteen miles southeast of town on the reservation, was instantly killed on Monday morning by being run over by a heavily loaded wagon. Mr. Brown accompained by L. A. Briggs, who is an employe of his son's, were about ten miles south of the ranch getting out logs for the construction of a new house. They started back early Monday morning with two heavy loads of logs. About half a mile from where they camped the road runs down into a canyon, and it was here the accident occurred. Mr. Briggs went down with his load first all right. He then went back to help the old gentleman down. One wheel was chained but the harness had no breeching and the load went down very fast at the bottom the team made a sharp turn running one wheel upon a ridge about two feet high and breaking the reach which precipitat-the front of the load to the ground. Mr. Brown was thrown off, the rear wheel running on and resting across his lungs, killing him instantly, or before the team could draw the load off. Mr. Briggs immediately saddled a horse and rode to the Geo. Brown home about ten miles away to notify the son and secure help, and returning the body was taken home. Funeral services were held at the home on Thursday and the remains were interred at the ranch. On behalf of the numerous friends of the family we extend sincerest sympathy to the bereaved ones.

Joseph Brown Death Notice, The Kadoka Press, June 26, 1908

On August 2, 1911, three years after the fatal accident of Joseph Brown, another tragic family death occurred. Joseph's son, George Brown, was killed by a lightning strike while riding his horse. The lightning bolt struck the rifle George was holding in his lap. His two older sons, George Jr. and Joe, were flanking him on either side and were unharmed.

George had all the qualities of a charismatic, trustworthy, and respectable individual, and his family, friends, acquaintances, and business associates in the Badlands community were sincerely saddened by his death. It was common knowledge that he was a good, honest man, and his obituary described him as "a man highly respected by all acquaintances and business associates, straightforward and honest, and his word was as good as a gold bond." Every family who lived in the area attended his funeral; the church was not large enough to hold all the mourners, and the funeral procession to his gravesite was over a mile in length.

Susie died on January 3, 1932, and although she remarried in the 1920s to Vetal Valandry, she was buried next to George, her one true love. Their graves are in Kadoka, South Dakota, in the Kadoka Calvary-Fairview Cemetery. They had nine children together.

George Brown Jr., born in 1894, married Clara Livermont.

Jennie Brown, born in 1895, married Joseph DeMarsche.

Joseph R. Brown., born in 1897, married Eloise Trimble.

Susie Brown, born in 1899, married Frank Bauman.

Anita Brown, born 1901, married Niels Terkildsen.

Leona Brown, born in 1903, married William Hauff. (My grandparents)

Florence Brown, born in 1905, married Stanley McCloskey.

Gloriette Brown, born in 1908, married Ross Banyard.

Thomas Brown, born in 1910, married Dorothy Morigeau.

GEORGE R. BROWN.

The news of the second tragedy of the day reached Kadoka about nine o'clock Wednesday evening when Geo. Brown, jr. road into town to summons help in their hour of sorrow.

Mr. Brown and his two sons were riding on the range, about nine miles from their home in the Red Stone Basin on the reservation. The eldest boy was riding a bronco and his father and brother were hazing the horse. Mr. Brown was only about ten feet away from the boys, and had just said 'Better pull up and let the horses rest a little,' when the lightning struck and killed him. The flash of lightning struck the horse on the side and Mr. Brown on the hip where the the rifle he was carrying rested, and followed through his body tearing his clothes into shreds and killing both himself and the horse. The boys were both shocked with the lightning and nearly knocked from their horses, but quickly recovering they hastened to their father's side to find that life was gone and that the lightning had set fire to the bosom of his shirt. This they extinguished and then rode home and got the spring wagon and brought the body to the house, and the eldest boy hastened to town with the sad tidings.

George R. Brown was a prominent horse raiser and has lived for years on the reservation, and was always held in the highest esteem by his hosts of friends, and it seems a pity that death should come in this manner and take him from our midst while in perfect health and the prime of manhood. A wife and family of nine children are survive him and have the the sympathy of all in this their hour of distress and sadness. No arrangemen have at this writing been made for the burial of the remains.

As mentioned earlier in the book, the Brown children, except for the youngest, Tom, attended Rapid City Indian School (RCIS). In my search for Grandma Leona Brown's enrollment records, I discovered data that puzzled me. Joseph R. Brown, the second son of George and Susie, was listed as one of the fifty children who died at the boarding school. The Brown family members were close, and I did not recall my dad mentioning that one of his uncles had died at the school. I searched the 1906-1916 enrollment records when Joseph attended. There was no other Joseph Brown enrolled at the school during that time. I contacted Amy Sazue, Executive Director of Remembering the Children, and Heather Dawn Thompson, Director of the Office of Tribal Relations for the Biden Administration. Both women encouraged me to pursue my investigation.

I continued to review the school records and family documents until I was confident that I had solved the puzzle. I had a photo of a middle-aged Joseph Brown with his wife, Eloise, and five children, Doris, Florence, Adele, Edwin, and Joe, so that was proof enough, but how did this error occur? While Joseph Brown most certainly had not died at the school, he had run away. In fact, he ran away many times. His father, George, sent a letter to the school telling them they should watch his son more closely. "Brown did not like children taking such risks and wanted to be sure they did not do so again."

Joseph would hop on the eastbound train as it left the Rapid City depot. The train passed by Belvidere close to the family ranch, where he would bail off and hide in the barn, asking his sisters to bring him food and water until his mother or father would discover him. The school documented him as a runaway in 1910, excused him for his father's death in 1911, excused him to go home after his brother had an accident in April 1912, and reported him as a deserter in December 1912. In 1913, at age 16, Joseph wrote a letter to the school asking if he could return, promising he would not run away again. The superintendent said he could come back because they needed him in the school band. Another time, the superintendent asked Joe to return because he was sorely needed for the upcoming football season.

In the RCIS records on child deaths, the cause of death for Joseph Brown is "[illegible] dead." I am guessing that the illegible word is "presumed." The records show his "death" in

1912 at age 14, the same year he deserted. In 2020, when a committee of volunteers assembled to investigate children's deaths that had occurred at the school, someone noted next to Joseph Brown's name, "This needs to be confirmed. It was difficult to read."

Children Who Passed Away at the Rapid City Indian Boarding School

Dozens of children passed away after being removed from their homes to attend the Rapid City Indian Boarding School. Most died from diseases to which they had little immunity, others died while attempting to run away from the school in the harsh South Dakota winter. The school did not keep complete records of the deceased, and many of the records were rendered illegible by the passage of time. This list is far from complete. But the painstaking hours of labor it took to compile this list is a small token from the authors in honor and memory of the children that never made it home:

[Illegible]	*Infant - Foreman**	*Martin Williamson*
Abner Kirk	*Infant - Naomi Goings**	*Mary Galligo*
Adolph Bissonettee	*Isadore Eagle Feather*	*Melania Rencountre*
Adolph Russell	*James Means*	*Nicholas Eagle Horn**
Alonzo Little Chief	*Jennie Pretends Eagle**	*Philip Moore*
*Bessie Bare Arm Necklace**	*John [Illegible]*	*Robert Cedar Boy*
Charles Crowdog	●*Joseph Brown*●	*Sophia Fleury*
Charles Long Turkey	*Joseph Face Darkling [Darling]*	*Spencer Ruff*
Dorothy Crier	*Josephine Spotted Bear*	*Susan Blue Horse**
Evelyn Day	*Lia Logan*	*Tommy Afraid of Thunder**
Female Child 1	*Louis Longhorn*	*Unnamed Child 1*
Female Child 2	*Luke Shell Necklace**	*Unnamed Child 2*
Female Child 3	*Mabel Holy**	*Unnamed Child 3*
Female Child 4	*Male Child 1*	*Unnamed Child 4*
Female Child 5	*Male Child 2*	*Unnamed Child 5*
Female Child 6	*Mark Sherman*	
Female Child 7	*Martin Hart*	

Indicates child is buried at the Mt. View Cemetery in Rapid City

After reconstructing the events, I contacted Remembering the Children, asking them to remove Joseph's name from the list of children who passed away. A meeting was called to review my documentation, and it was agreed that the death of Joseph Brown at Rapid City Indian School was indeed an error. I do not blame anyone for this error; after all, the inaccuracy occurred over one hundred years ago. I thank the people who worked on this project. Fortunately, Joseph Rooks Brown lived a good life until 1951 when he died suddenly from a heart attack.

Rapid City Indian Boarding School
Child Deaths
Last Updated 10/4/2020

	Date	Name	Age	Cause	Tribe	Other Info
9.	February 18, 1917	Alonzo Little Chief	16	"Died."	Cheyenne	Cheyenne
10.	April 18, 1917	Joseph Brown	14	"[illegible] dead"	Oglala	¼ blood "Excused April 11, 1912 on account of accident to brother." 14 on April 11, 1912 This needs to be confirmed. It was difficult to read.
11.	May 15, 1917	Luke Shell Necklace	17	"Died"	Cheyenne River Sioux	A hospital report during this time listing patients, births, and deaths, reported the deaths of two male children. It did not list a cause of death. **Buried at Mountain View Cemetery:** May 18, 1917 Luke Shell Necklace (Row 62 - RCIS Plot 11; MV 62-895-11)
12.	May 19, 1917	Martin Hart	17	"Died"	Cheyenne	A hospital report during this time listing patients, births, and deaths, reported the deaths of two male children. It did not list a cause of death.
13.	September 1, 1917	Joseph Face Darkling	14	"Died."	Rosebud	Full blood Other children named Sam and Laura with the same last name attended in the same time period. Sometimes the name is listed as Face Darling.
14.	September 1, 1917	Martin Williamson	13	"Died."	Yankton	½ blood
15.	September 30, 1917	Mary Galligo	18	"Died."	Oglala	½ blood
16.	October 23, 1918	Josephine Spotted Bear	17	"Died"	Standing Rock	Likely Spanish Flu. This was during the height of the Spanish Flu. A doctor's report from the school files states that 9 children dies in the second and third quarters from "influenza." It states that it was two boys and seven girls but does not name them.
17.	November 10, 1918	Melissa Rencountre	16	"Died"	Lower Brule	(Might be "Melania") Likely Spanish Flu. This was during the height of the Spanish Flu. A doctor's report from the school files states that 9 children died in the second and third quarters from "influenza". It states that it was two boys and seven girls but does not name them.

6

Mr. J. F. House
Rapid City So. D.

Belvidere
South. Dak.
September 17, 1913.

Dear Sir:
I will drop you a line in order to ask you if you want me to finish this next year, my term is not out yet. I have one more year to attend that school so if you want me to come I'll come and stay the whole year, and I'll make it a promise that I'll not run away again it has been kind of Rainy down this way the last couple days so we couldent do any thing at all.

I am yours truly
Joseph R Brown.

abress Belvidere
So. Da.

P.S. write to me at once Because I want to start right away.

Rapid City School, S. D.,
Sept. 20, 1913.

Mr. Joseph R. Brown,
Belvidere, S. D.

Dear Sir:
Your letter is received and I note that you wish to come back to school. I am willing for you to come here but you must come with the understanding that you cannot leave until the close of the school year. We would be very glad to have you and especially need you in the band but you understand the discipline of the school and I know that you can comply with all that is desired. I shall be very glad to help you and ff you make an honest effort know you will be much benefited by coming back.

Respectfully,

H/M   Superintendent.

Quarterly Report, June 30, 1910. Joe R. Brown, Age 12, Pine Ridge, SD.
The note on the far right reads: Ran away & returned in quarter.

Name	Age	Tribe	Agency or reservation	Date	Grade	Detail or occupation	Number...	Average daily attendance	Remarks
Adams, Benj.	17	Sioux	Pine Ridge	1911.	5 6	Tailor Shop	25	92	
Arrow, Arthur T.	17	"	Yankton	1911	7 8	Dormitory	10	50	
Black Hat, Thomas	17	"	Standing Rock	1911	1 2	Engineer	20	92.	
Bad Horse, Ernest	18	"	Lower Brule	9/17/12	4 4	Shoe Shop.	16	92	
Boyer, Mitchel	15	"	Pine Ridge	9/25/12	3 3	Kitchen	14	92	
" , Sam	10	"	"	9/25/12	1 1	To Small for Detail	14	92	
Bottle, Daniel	15	"	"	9/30/12	4 4	Dormitory	25	92	
Brave Heart, Moses	17	"	"	1911	4 4	Farm	30	91	
Brings Yellow, James	16	"	"	1911	2A 2A	Kitchen	5	89	
" , Charles	11	"	"	1911	2B 2B	To Small for Detail	5	89	
Brave Plenty, Daniel	11	"	Cheyenne River R.E.	10/7/12	2A 2A	Domestic Science	1	86	
" , Hobson	16	"	"	1911	6 6	Dormitory	1	85	
Blue Bird, John	17	"	Rosebud	10/10/12	4 4	Farm	4	87	
Bad Moccasin, Cooke	19	"	Crow Creek	1910	6 6	Engineer	15	76	
Boyer, James	10	"	Pine Ridge	1911	2 2	Not Detailed	40	80	
Brown, Joseph	15	"	"	1911	5 6	Farm	30	48	*Deserter.
Black Horse, Francis	15	"	Rosebud	1910	2 3A	Farm	20	70	
Cottier, Edward	16	"	Pine Ridge	1910	5A 7	Tailor Shop	20	92	
" , Benj.	12	"	"	1910	1 1A	Kitchen	20	92	
Gray Thunder, Joseph	18	"	Pine Ridge	1911	4A 5B	Carpenter	35	92	
Clifford, William	16	"	"	1910	5 5B	Dormitory	9	92	
" , Robert	13	"	"	1909	1 3A	"	9	92	
Crabe, Adam	10	"	Cheyenne River	R.E. 1912.	1 2	Janitor	8	92	
" , Joseph	16	"	"	R.E. 1912	1 4A	"	8	92	
Clifford, Henry	14	"	Pine Ridge	1911	3A 3A	Farm	25	92	
Condon, Silas	14	"	Cheyenne River	R.E. 1912	1 4A	Janitor	32	85	
Chips, Joseph	11	"	Pine Ridge	10/26/12	1 1	Not Detailed	12	65	
" , Dallis	14	"	"	10/26/12	3B 5B	Janitor	12	65	
Clifford, George	17	"	"	1.11	5A 5A	Carpenter	15	29	
Deon, Harold	15	"	"	1911	5 4	Dormitory	6	92	

2459

Joseph Brown, Age 15, was reported as a deserter.

William and Leona (Brown) Hauff

I was never particularly interested in reading about World Wars I and II, but Grandpa Hauff's involvement captivated me, sending me down the rabbit hole of research. Dad spoke very little about it, only rudimentary facts when I questioned him, and he never used the word "hero" when discussing his father's military service. However, it is evident that William Hauff was a hero, a staunch patriot who was passionate about serving his country in times of war. He was incredibly courageous and put his life on the line probably more times than we will ever know. Enlisting as a private in 1917 and discharged from the United States Army with the rank of Major in 1956, he participated in two of the bloodiest wars in history, and no matter how high his rank, he did not dodge combat, fighting on the front lines until age 44. He served with three of the most distinguished military divisions in American history—The 1st Infantry Division in WWI, the elite 508th Parachute Infantry Regiment, and the 82nd Airborne Division in WWII. Basic training for the 508th was physically and mentally intense, eliminating many men, but those who made it through the rigorous instruction were soldiers of the highest caliber.

My dad was somewhat bitter about what he viewed as his father's abandonment, and considering his mother's fragile health and steady decline, this is understandable. He was seventeen when his mother passed, on the verge of manhood, raised in a government boarding school with his father frequently absent from home, and he looked to his mother as the only source of unconditional love. One can imagine the traumatizing effect that her death had upon him and his siblings. I believe that is why his writings ended where they did; it was too painful for him to recollect and continue.

William A. Hauff enlisted in the legendary 1st Infantry Division, known as "The Big Red One." He was an original Doughboy, departing in 1917 with one of the first units that sailed from New York City to St. Nazaire, France. After a brief stay in rest camps, the privates began training in Paris, overseen by Captain George S. Patton.

William A. Hauff's World War I helmet, "Big Red One."

On October 23, 1917, the first American shell of World War I was fired at German lines by a 1st Infantry Division unit. By April 1918, the Germans had pushed to within 40 miles of Paris, and The Big Red One moved in to assist the battle-fatigued French First Army. The U.S. 28th Infantry Regiment followed the 1st Infantry Division, attacking the town and capturing 250 German soldiers. It was the first American victory in World War I.

Private William Hauff, center, WWI, 1919

William Hauff kept a diary during WWI, from December 1, 1918, through July 15, 1919. It is quite extraordinary to read. On the first page, Dec. 1, he writes, "We hiked the hardest day hike that was remembered by us since or after. We came to Konz, but no room to spare so we hiked up the river to the next village by the name of Filz where we were billeted overnight. The first night in Germany was one to be remembered "beaucoup" guards." They hiked 10 to 16 hours daily in German territory that winter through mud and slush up to their knees. At one point, they went for two days without a meal because the kitchen squad got lost.

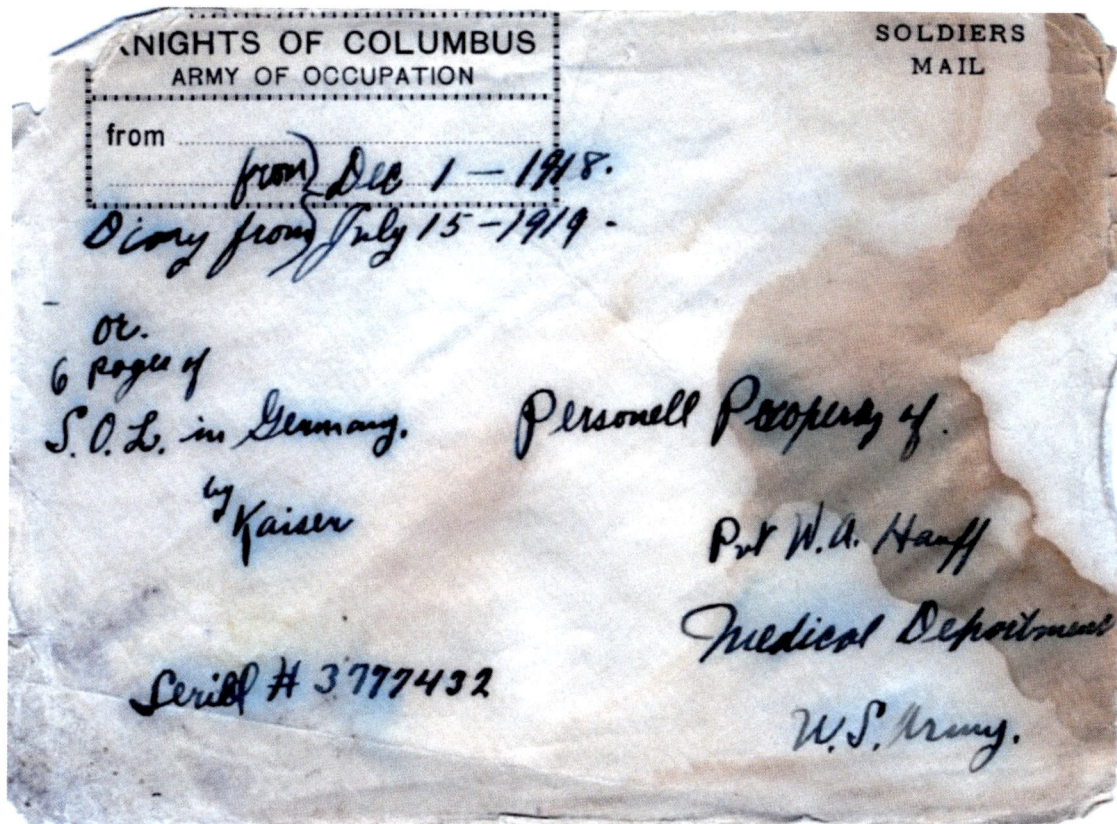

KNIGHTS OF COLUMBUS

Army of Occupation

History #part II

Page #1.

Dec. 1 1918. The 1st Div. was a part of the 3rd Army. or Army of Occupation, and assigned to take and hold the Coblenz Bridge head, and were sent in lead of all other divisions. We started to hike the first day. rainy, drizzly, and mud over the shoe tops. We hiked to Grevenmacher Luxemburg where we passed over the mosselle on a bridge which but 4 days ago carried german soldiers across. to Germany. The civilians were surprised at american troops and big crowds gather in the villages to take a peek at those americans. We hiked the hardest day hike that was remember by us since or after. We came to "Konz" but no room to spare so we hiked up the river to the next village. by the name of Filzem where we were billeted over night. The first night in Germany was one to be remembered "beaucoup" guards.

Dec. 2 Hiked all day passing through "Treier" or "Treves" at 11. A.M. hiked along railroad track. and moselle. River all day at night stopped at Fell.

Dec. 3. Hiked all day at 6.30 came to Neumagen, where we were forced to stop over night its was cold and raining.

Dec. 4. Hiked all day at night came to a small village named. Bürgen where we stayed all night. Orders had been issued that every man must carry full pack and no straggling allowed before the hike started.

Dec. 5. Hiked from 4.30 A.M. to 10.30 P.M. no eats kitchens are lost. stayed at Kinheim.

Dec. 6 Hiked all day no eats. at night about 10.30 Kitchens come into camp no eats. village A lodgund

Dec. 7. Good Breakfast. ??? you know. everything tasted good. Hiked to 1.30 P.M. crossed moselle on Ferry Boat. Hiked to 5.30 when we came to Finkel where we stayed Dec 8. it being Sunday.

Dec. 9. Hiked to Bürgen 29 Kilos.

Dec. 10 Hiked to Waldesch. near Coblenz and the country is beautiful. a 28. Kilo Hike.

Dec. 11. waited at. Waldesch for Germans to clear out Coblenz and Bridge Head vicinity

December. 12. at 1.30. A.M. rolled packes and assembled ready to hike.

3

KNIGHTS OF COLUMBUS

Army of Occupation

at 4.30 A.M. started for Coblenz. at 10.30 Hiked into main city top to the Kaiser's Ring with Bands playing and full colors. We were reviewed by French and British Generals also American Officers. We were billeted for the night in an empty building call the Festhalle 1st Batt 28th Inf. and room for more. We expected to stay in Coblenz for a while but our dreams were false for early next morning at 5.30 We were up. and on Dec. 13. at 7.15 We crossed the German Rhine. on the span bridge near the Fest halls. Raining, Pitchforks Bands playing and troops cursing Rain my God rain and mud till Hell wouldn't have it but rave on. We hiked in slush and mud over our Knees as the roads were soft and the German artillery had just pass ahead of us about 2 days ago. At night We stopped in Dern back. We were billeted in a Gymnasium cold. wet, and hungry. no bunks.

Dec. 14. got up early. at 10.30 hiked about 14 Kilos to. Ruppach. where we were stationed for some time.

KNIGHTS OF COLUMBUS

Army of Occupation

Dec. 15. was made orderly and Dental Asst.
for Capt. Cloutier. Dental Corps U. S. Army.
Dec 21. The Infirmary was moved to Goldhausen
not very far from Ruppach. but the Capt. and
myself stayed in Ruppach.
Dec. 25 for Xmas got a Christmas box from the
Y. M. C. A. containing 1 br. chock. bar. 1 pk ciggettes
1 cigar 1 can of Velvet Smoking tobacco 1 pk cakes.
From the kitchen we were served all good things to
eat pork, and more chock late
Dec. 26 Drawed my November pay of frances 145.00
in German money. 241. marks.
Dec. 24. Seen my first snow in Europe; not much.
Dec 31. Silvester evening celebrated with the people
of the house being the bürgermeister of Ruppach.
"Departe" 1918. Entree. 1919
1. Jan Celebrated with people of house very fine
people also have a very fine girl.
Jan 16. Drawed my December pay which was
216 mks.
Jan. 19. Moved to 3rd Batt. 28th with outfit.
which was stationed in Wallmerod and Molsberg

KNIGHTS OF COLUMBUS

Army of Occupation

#5

Castle on outpost duty.

Jan. 22 signed pay roll. for month of Jan of which I deposited $26.00.

Jan 27. got a pass to Coblenz 12 hr. took boat trip on steamer Borussia first Excursion of its kind on the Rhine Up River and back.

Jan 31. 3rd Batt is relieved from outpost duty and move back to Heiligenroth on

Feb. 1. 1919.

Feb. 3. pay day drawed 35 Francs.

Feb. 15 got sick. and was sent to Field Hospital #3 in Dernbach Influenza.

Feb 22 returned to 3rd Battalion to duty.

Feb. 23 Recieved my first letter since I was in Europe and that was from mother. I missed signing the pay roll for month of Feb. while in hospital so no pay day.

March. 14. Had a big review of 1st Div. Seen General Pershing for first time.

April. 4 drawed two months pay or 30 F Francs.

May. 4 drawed 1 month pay. 253. mks.

~~May 5 or [illegible]~~

130

KNIGHTS OF COLUMBUS

Army of Occupation

On May 16 was order from 3rd Batt. to Regimental Hqas. with Dental outfit. Set up outfit. Village of Mendt.

May 18th signed pay roll for month of May.

June. 8. quit Capt Cloutier and am going to school, and drilling.

June 10. received pass to Paris 3 day. furlough.

June 19 came back from Paris order to alert position as Germans refuse to sign peace. Troops concentration position to at Fütchbach. 14 Kilo from Mendt. Outpost duty now.

June. 28. relieved from alert position moved to Berod.

June. 29. moved to Dembach. I was attached first aid 1st Batt. during alert position Co. B.

July. 3. was taken back to Mendt. go to school drill.

July. 4 celebrated Horse Show in Montabaur

July 10-11 on K.P.

July 12-14 went to Circus at Montabaur, 1st Div. Circus very good time.

William A. Hauff, Cavalry, Ft. Riley

William A. Hauff, participating in an equestrian competition at Ft. Riley, Kansas.

William A. Hauff, 2nd Row, Fifth from Right

William A. Hauff with his sons
Left to right: William, Billie, Dick, and Sylvan wearing his dad's Cavalry hat.

When the United States entered World War II after the bombing of Pearl Harbor, Hauff reenlisted with the 508th Parachute Infantry Regiment (PIR), known as "The Red Devils."

508th Parachute Infantry Regiment

Home		Up	CIB (Ha - Har)	CIB (Harr - Hen)	CIB (Her - Hol)

CIB (Hoo - Hyd)

RANK	SURNAME	FORENAMES	EFF DATE	COMPANY	SOURCE
Pfc	Harrelson	Walter W	France	Posthumous	GO-31
Pvt	Harris	Guy S	10 Feb 1945	Co I	GO-8
T/5	Harris	Jeff	6 Jun 1944	APO 230	GO-50
Pvt	Harris	William H	10 Mar 1945	HQ 2nd	GO-8
Pvt	Harris	Willis E	10 Mar 1945	Co D	GO-8
Pvt	Harrison	Ollie R	15 Feb 1945	Co D	GO-8
Sgt	Harrold	Joseph J	France	Posthumous	GO-31
Pfc	Hart	Robert W	14 Sep 1944	Co B	GO-56
Sgt	Hartman	Clare G	6 Jun 1944	APO 230	GO-50
T/4	Hartman	Elek	11 Aug 1944	Co B	GO-50
Pvt	Hartman	George E	Holland	Posthumous	GO-31
Pvt	Hartzell	William J	10 Mar 1945	Co F	GO-8
2/Lt	Hauff	William A	6 Jun 1944	?	GO-50
Capt	Harvey	Wayne K	France	Posthumous	GO-31
Pfc	Haskett	Paul A	6 Jun 1944	APO 230	GO-50
Pfc	Hass	Robert L	10 Mar 1945	HQ 3rd	GO-8
Pvt	Haste	William K	France	Posthumous	GO-31
Pfc	Hatcher	Francis M	10 Mar 1945	Co G	GO-8
Pvt	Hattrick	James R	France	Posthumous	GO-31
2/Lt	Hauff	William A	6 Jun 1944	APO 230	GO-50
2/Lt	Havens	Robert N	6 Jun 1944	APO 230	GO-50
Pvt	Havens	Victory F	Holland	Posthumous	GO-31
Sgt	Hayes	Wendell E	6 Jun1944	France	GO-38
T/4	Hazy	John D	6 Jun 1944	APO 230	GO-50
Pvt	Head	Curtis P	6 Jun 1944	Hq 1st	GO-50
Pvt	Headington	Jerome W	10 Mar 1945	Co C	GO-8
Pvt	Heinz	Albert L	France	Posthumous	GO-31
Pvt	Helmick	Gale D	10 Feb 1945	Co I	GO-8
Sgt	Helton	Delbert A	France	Posthumous	GO-31
Pvt	Hempton	Herman E	17 Sep 1944	Co A	GO-13
Cpl	Henderson	Alvin H	6 Jun 1944	[Not stated]	GO-54
Cpl	Henderson	Alvin H	14 Sep 1944	Co A	GO-56
Pfc	Hendrickson	Thomas G	10 Mar 1945	Co A	GO-8
SSgt	Henry	David A	France	Posthumous	GO-31

On June 6, 1944, Hauff participated in D-Day. The airborne assault preceded the amphibious assault. 10,000 American air troops and 14,000 Allied air troops were dropped behind enemy lines before 132,000 men landed on the five beaches of Normandy. The gliders flew through heavy clouds, and the 508th PIR jumped amidst a heavy concentration of Anti-Aircraft (AA) and Machine Gun (MG) fire. Because of the poor visibility, the 508th became scattered, and many parachutists missed their landing mark and had to scramble to regroup. They fought for the next 34 days; some were taken as prisoners of war, and many were killed. The 508th PIR would remain attached to the 82nd Airborne Division for the remainder of the war.

The manual, Der Dienftunterricht im heere, which translates to "Service Instruction in the Army," was found in 2019 in an army trunk stored in the rafters of Sylvan's garage. The chest also included William Hauff's war medals, WWI helmet, WWII uniform, a Hitler Youth Bronze medal, war maps, and coins from Germany, France, Belgium, Holland, and Korea.

The Hitler Youth Badge was instituted in 1934 as an incentive to improve the physical and ideological proficiency of the growing membership of the Hitler Youth. It required participation in the study of ideology and weekly attendance at meetings. All members were issued a performance book (Leistungsbuch) to record their achievements and as a certificate of proficiency.

Hitler Youth Proficiency Badge (H J Leistungsabzeichen) found in William Hauff's Army trunk.

REIBERT

William A. Hauff
Dr. Ens.

Der Dienst-
Unterricht
im Heere

Ausgabe für den
Schützen der
Schützenkompanie

Zusammengestellt und bearbeitet
von

Dr. jur. W. Reibert
Hauptmann u. Kompaniechef

Mit über 500 Abbildungen im Text
und 10 mehrfarbigen Tafeln

Elfte, völlig neubearbeitete Auflage

Jahrgang 1938/39

E. S. Mittler & Sohn, Berlin

Captured at
Vin de Fontaine   Bruno

Front Cover

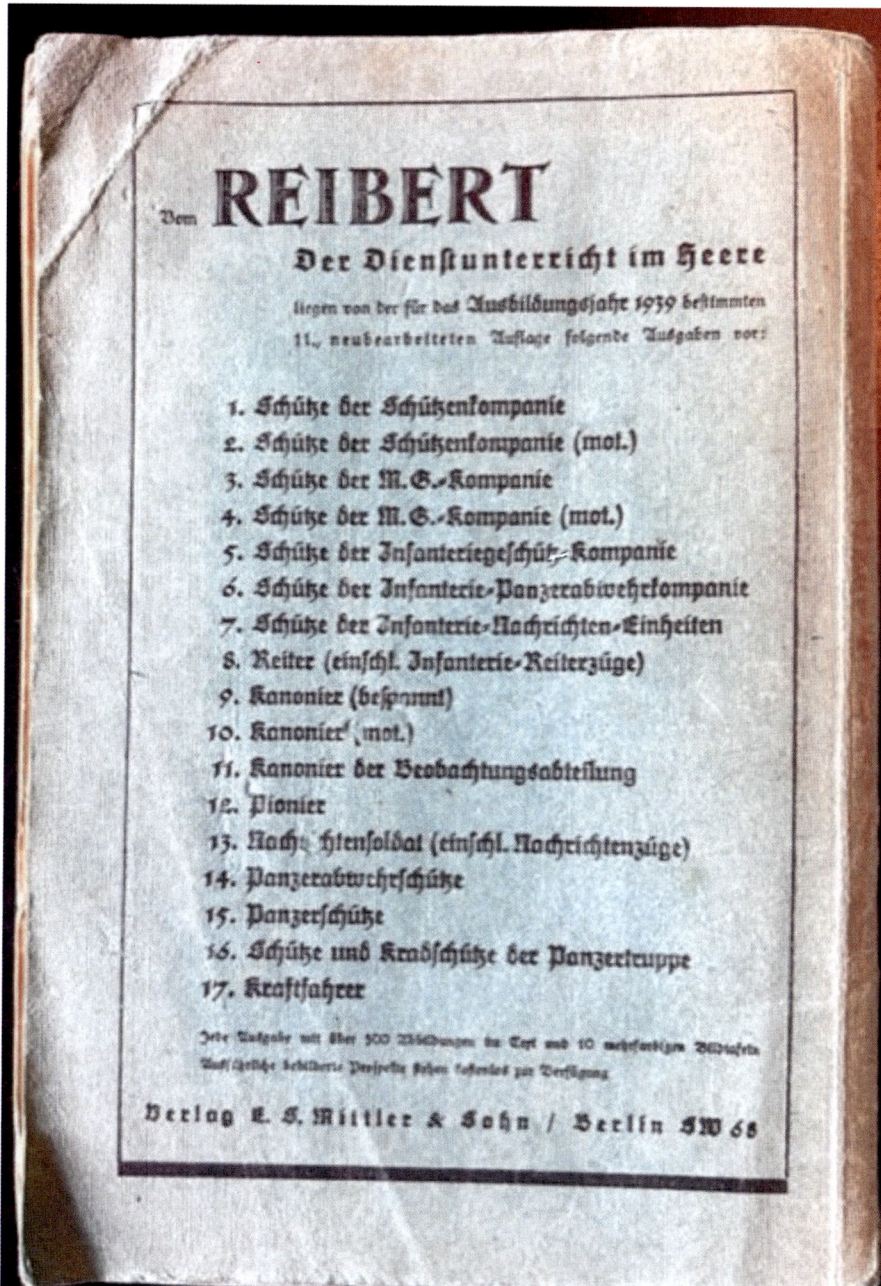

Der **REIBERT**

Der Dienstunterricht im Heere

liegen von der für das Ausbildungsjahr 1939 bestimmten
11., neubearbeiteten Auflage folgende Ausgaben vor:

1. Schütze der Schützenkompanie
2. Schütze der Schützenkompanie (mot.)
3. Schütze der M.G.-Kompanie
4. Schütze der M.G.-Kompanie (mot.)
5. Schütze der Infanteriegeschütz-Kompanie
6. Schütze der Infanterie-Panzerabwehrkompanie
7. Schütze der Infanterie-Nachrichten-Einheiten
8. Reiter (einschl. Infanterie-Reiterzüge)
9. Kanonier (bespannt)
10. Kanonier (mot.)
11. Kanonier der Beobachtungsabteilung
12. Pionier
13. Nachrichtensoldat (einschl. Nachrichtenzüge)
14. Panzerabwehrschütze
15. Panzerschütze
16. Schütze und Kradschütze der Panzertruppe
17. Kraftfahrer

Jede Ausgabe mit über 500 Abbildungen im Text und 10 mehrfarbigen Bildtafeln
Ausführliche bebilderte Prospekte stehen kostenlos zur Verfügung

Verlag E. S. Mittler & Sohn / Berlin SW 68

Back Cover and Spine

Reibert / Dienstunterricht Schütze der Schützenkompanie 11. Aufl. 1938/39

Der Führer und Reichskanzler
Adolf Hitler
Oberster Befehlshaber der Deutschen Wehrmacht

William A. Hauff
Lt. Cav.

Inside Cover Page Translation:
The German Chancellor, Head of the Third Reich
Adolf Hitler
Supreme Commander of the Unified Armed Forces of the Third Reich

Translation:
Top: Hermann Göring, Third Reich Minister of Aviation and Commander-in-Chief of Air Force
Middle Left: Wilhelm Keitel, Commander-in-Chief of the Armed Forces of the Third Reich
Middle Right: Walther von Brauchitsch, Commander-in-Chief of the Army
Bottom: Erich Raeder, Grand Admiral Commander-in-Chief of the Navy

All four commanders pictured above were charged with war crimes when the war ended. Göring, one of the most powerful military officers in the Nazi Party, and Keitel were both denied their requests for a military execution by firing squad. Göring committed suicide by cyanide the night before his hanging, and Keitel was hanged as scheduled. Brauchitsch died of pneumonia in October of 1948 before he was tried in Nüremberg. Raeder, who held the highest possible rank in the German Navy, was sentenced to life in prison but was released in 1955 due to ailing health. He died in 1960.

Hauff wrote: "Captured at Vin de Fontaine France" with a fountain pen on the front cover of the manual. Only one notable skirmish took place in this region. I believe the battle below was where Lieutenant Colonel William A. Hauff captured a Nazi soldier and came into possession of Der Dienftunterricht im heere.

Battery Firing Record – June 20,1944, D+14

On the morning of June 20th, the remainder of the **82nd Airborne Division** arrived at Pretot, with the 507th PIR, **the 508th PIR**, and the 505th PIR all taking up positions on the flanks of the 325th GIR. Each regiment tried to expand the new bridgehead over the Douve River and create more room for the American infantry divisions coming up from the Omaha and Utah beaches. It was also on this date that the men of the 82nd Airborne Division adopted the unofficial motto "no quarter asked, no quarter given." This new motto was in response to news of the slaughter of injured 82nd paratroopers by a unit of the Waffen SS on June 6th, in the French village of Graignes. From now on, it would be a fight to the death between the Nazis (the SS storm troopers) and the 82nd Airborne, in every encounter where these two elite fighting units faced each other.

At 1000 hours Major Todd received orders from division headquarters to move to a new position so that the 319th could provide fire support to all active airborne regiments in the field. According to this new communique, the 325th had reached the bridge at coordinates 25.8.87.8, and immediately to the left of this position the 508th was dug in near Vin de Fontaine. To the right of the 325th was the 507th near Baupte, while the 505th was placed in reserve at the rear of this combat zone, ready to respond at a moment's notice if there was an enemy breakthrough. Because of the superiority of the Allied air forces over the skies of Normandy, Major Todd decided to take advantage of this factor and use Piper "Cub" observation planes to improve the observation perspective for the forward artillery observer teams. Each forward observer from this date onward would spend some time in a Piper Cub, on a rotating basis, observing German positions for the 319 batteries. At 2200 hours of June 20, 1944, all batteries reported ready for action in their new positions.

~ Silent Wings Savage Death: Saga of the 82nd Airborne's Glider Artillery in WWII ~

William Hauff squatting, second from left. Photo taken in Paris, France, 1944.
Arc de Triomphe after the liberation of Paris from the Nazis.

Hauff continued to see action as an Intelligence Officer with the 82nd Airborne Division in Normandy, Holland, Belgium, and Germany. Following the Second World War, he served as the Commander at a German Prisoner of War (POW) camp in Colorado. He spoke fluent German and communicated flawlessly with the prisoners. When the German POWs were released, Hauff accompanied some back to their homeland of Germany.

William Hauff wrote many letters from Europe during World War II, and his close friends, the Greeks, kept them to share with his family. He could never disclose his location and would write, "Somewhere in England" or "Somewhere in Belgium."

Elvin greek
Caroline g.

Emma g. Leona H. Bill H. Eula g.
Rachel g. Sylvan Hauff Laura g.
Richard H. •Luella H.

This photo was taken of the Greek and Hauff families at a picnic along the White River, Todd County, South Dakota, c. 1938. Before WWII.

Here are some letters written by a dear family friend, Bill Hauff,to Perry and Emma Greek, during and soon after WWII.

In August, 1998, I talked on the telephone with Bill's youngest son, Sylvan Hauff in Rapid City, SD, and acquired some additonal information about the family. I wrote up the following from our conversation and later Sylvan corrected and added to it.

Bill's parents, Johannes and Maria Hauf, were Germans from Russia. Their ancestors had migrated to Russia and settled in the Ukraine and Volga River (Saratov), areas at the invitation of Catherine the Great, a century earlier. They were educated in Russia and Johannes' family was considered to be fairly well off there. John (as he preferred to be called) learned English easily and could read and write in German, Russian and English; his wife learned to speak the English language but could read and write only in German.

John could read and write English well enough to qualify as a letter carrier. He added an "F" to his last name because there was another John Hauf in the area and their mail was often mixed up.

They first settled in Butte County, near Naper, Nebraska, where they homesteaded. Later they moved over the border into Gregory County, SD, where they operated a store south of Dallas, SD, and were also engaged in farming. Still later, prior to WWI, they owned a ranch northwest of Okreek, SD.

There were nine children in the family: John; Anna, who married Henry Hafner; John Carl, who went by Carl, married Elizabeth and farmed near Witten; Fred, who worked in the steel mills around Chicago; Jake, who married Alvina, called "Viney" lived in Parmelee and Rapid City and their children were Lester, Dolores, Arlene, Shirley and Violet; Edward; Walter, the youngest married Iona White and lived in Idaho; Ida married Herb Sunding; and and William (Bill), who was born in 1900.

John and Maria (who preferred to be called Mary) were neighbors to Perry and Emma Greek when they lived northwest of Mission. Mrs. Hauff assisted when Lester and Daniel were born in 1920 and 1921. They also lived east Parmelee at one time, and finally in Rapid City, where both are buried.

Bill got his education of six years, at a Lutheran School taught in German, so German was his first language. He volunteered for WWI, served as an Army Medic in Europe; was commissioned as a Second Lieutenant and stayed in the Reserve for a while. After discharge, he worked for Homestake Mining Company in Lead, SD, and later engaged in trucking with Shorty Reifel at Rosebud. Later he began farming and ranching.

Bill married Leona Brown in 1923, at Lead, SD. They had four children: William (Billie), Richard (Dick), Sylvan and Luella. They lived at various places, ranching at Norris and Parmelee.

Leona had a very interesting background. She was born along Cut Meat Creek at Parmelee in 1903 where her parents ran an Indian Trading Post. Her maternal grandfather was Joseph O. Rooks, Sr., who served as a Union soldier in the Civil War. He was an early Pony Express Rider in Colorado, married an Indian lady named "Tingleska" (meaning fawn) and had three children. One of the children was Susie Rooks, who was one-half Indian. She married George Brown who was one-quarter Indian. Leona was one of their nine children who were 3/8ths Indian.

George Racine Brown, Leona's father, was born at Fort Collins, Colorado, became a registered Indian Trader on the Rosebud Indian Reservation and had a Trading Post at Cut Meat, which they sold in about 1906 to the Thode family of Belvidere, SD. The family moved to a ranch in the Red Stone Basin of the Bad Lands area.

George attended school at the Carlisle Institute at Carlisle, PA, for six years. The legendary Jim Thorpe also attended Carlisle Institute. Later George went with the Buffalo Bill Cody's Wild West show as a trick rider and roping expert.

Leona received her education at the Rapid City Indian School. She went by train from Belvidere, north of the Red Stone Basin. In the summer of 1911, Leona's father was riding horseback between his two young sons, when he was struck by lightning and killed. Her mother continued to operate the ranch for several years after that. As a child, Leona suffered from rheumatic fever and from about 1939 on, suffered and was often hospitalized with heart problems. The childhood rheumatic fever had damaged a valve in her heart.

Bill and Leona moved from their Washabaugh County ranch to Parmelee in about 1938. In 1941, they moved to Rapid City.

Soon after Pearl Harbor in 1942, Bill enlisted in the Army as a Private. He was sent to OCS and commissioned as an officer. He was sent to an Army Intelligence School, at Carlisle Barracks, PA, interestingly, the site of the old Carlisle Institute. Later, he completed paratrooper training in England and was assigned to the 82nd AirBorne Division as an Intelligence Officer. He must have been a remarkable physical specimen as he was in a tough outfit, the 508th Parachute Regiment for the invasion at Normandy and the Battle of the Bulge in Belgium, and later was assigned to the 325th Glider Regiment of the liberation of Holland.

Bill spoke fluent German and part of his duties in military intelligence was the interrogation of German Prisoners of War. Some of those men were able to identify the area of Germany from which Bill's parents had probably migrated, which was Swabia or Baden Wertenberg.

After the War, Bill was the Commamndant at a German POW camp at Walden, Colorado. Later he made several trips escorting POW's back to Germany.

Then he was assigned to a Military Goverment group in Korea, where he was stationed at the time of Leona's death in March, 1947, at Rapid City, SD. There at Taejon (Korea) the group deisgned and built water and sewer systems which had been destroyed by the Japanese. All of this was later destroyed again by the North Koreans in the Korean War.

After returning from Korea, Bill reverted back to a permanent rank and was assigned to a Quartermaster Remount Station at Fort Robinson, Nebraska, which was closed in 1950. From there, he transferred to Fort Riley, Kansas.

2

Bill was married a second time to Golda Cowell Brown in 1948. She was a county officer in Bennett County, Martin, SD. Golda died of cancer in 1951 at Fort Riley.

Bill came back to Martin and held the office of County Auditor and County Treasurer. He died in 1963 from heart trouble and emphysema.

Sylvan recalled fond memories of Parmelee. He remembers helping Elvin and Shorty put up hay and oats down on our farm. He also went with Elvin to the farm where they caught giant bull frogs, put them in a barrel and transported them to Eagle Feather Dam, where after they were established we would go out and shoot them and the Hauff boys would dive in to get them. (The Greek kids couldn't swim.) Sylvan says he has eaten Frog Legs at several restaurants since then but none ever tasted as good as those from the Eagle Feather Dam. Sylvan thinks that Dad (Perry Greek) had those frog eggs imported from Missouri.

He remembers Elvin taking our new car out on the newly paved Highway 18, southwest of town, and driving 90 miles an hour!!! Sylvan says he had some good meals at Mrs. Greek's table. He and Shorty had some good times together, even developing a code system where if Shorty honked an old horn a certain number of times, that was a signal for Sylvan to come on over to our house, which was only a block away. He also remembered the make-shift shower we had in a corner of our wash house. It was a tank about four foot across that they put on top of the roof next to the windmill and pumped water into it. It warmed up during the day and in the evening, we could have a shower. Very modern!!!

Sylvan at the age of six, as did the other children in the family, left home to attend school at the Pine Ridge Boarding School. He tells of a regimented life, all dressing alike, eating and sleeping in large rooms, being treated well--but that it was mighty lonely for a six-year old. Their leather shoes were made at the Federal Prison at Fort Leavenworth, KS, and the wool suits they wore on Sundays were made at the Federal Prison in Terre Haute, Indiana. The remarkable thing is that he relates this without bitterness but knowing that it was the best his parents could do for him at that time.

Sylvan was born -------30 at ---.
Sylvan graduated from the University of South Dakota in 1953. He was commissioned a Second Lieutenant in the Army through ROTC and spent some time in Germany. He began employment as a Federal Probation and Parole Officer in Sioux Falls in December, 1956, and became the Chief Probation Officer for the District of South Dakota, a position he held until his retirement in November, 1984. Later he was self-employed as a Private Investigator and legal assistant at a Rapid City law firm.

Interestingly enough, two of his parolees were the two young part-Indian men, Stanley Hatten and Herb Bonser, who were convicted and sent to life in prison at Leavenworth, KS, for the murder in 1931 of Mr. Dowling at the store in Parmelee. They hid out around Tuthill, SD and had cut a telephone line west of Parmelee.

After release from Prison, Hatten became an alcoholic and broke his parole a couple times. Bonser was a taxi-driver in Rapid City for many years, neither of them ever committed violent acts

3

again. Two older white men were also involved in the murder.
They were established criminals and one was later killed in a
prison fight. All four men were armed during the robbery and
none ever confessed to being the killer.

Sylvan married Margaret Skalinder of Martin, SD, (they were
childhood sweethearts from boarding school days) and adopted her
three children from an earlier marriage. They had four
additional children, for a total of seven.

Their children are April Kaye Gustafson of Rapid City; Steven
Anthony Hauff of Spearfish; Tracy Dahlgren of Rapid City; Echo
Rust of Rapid City; Alison Dawn Strauss of Rapid City; The
Reverend Bradley Sylvan Hauff, an Episcopal Priest in St. Paul,
MN; and Brian Hauff of Rapid City.

William (Billie) Hauff was born 10-26-25 at Parmelee SD.
He graduated from the University of SD in 1950 and worked as an
engineer with the US Bureau of Indian Affairs many years and in
various locations. He died of a heart attack in Phoenix, AZ, in
1976 while stationed at Coolidge, AZ, as a supervising highway
engineer. Billie served aboard a Navy LST as a radioman during
World War II.

Richard (Dick) Hauff was born 1-13-28 at Rosebud, SD.
He graduated from Black Hills State College in Industrial Arts
and worked as a teacher and Public Health Educator for the US
Indian Health Service. He died in August, 1997, after a long
battle with cardiac problems. Dick served as a combat
infantryman in Korea.

Luella (Hauff) Torres was born 6-10-32 at Norris, SD.
She graduated from the Pennsylvania Hospital School of Nursing in
Philadelphia and worked many years as a registered nurse for the
US Indian Health Service. She had ten children and was the
Director of Nursing at the Sioux San PHS Hospital in Rapid City
prior to her death.

* * * * * * * * * * * *

I remember the Hauff family when they lived in Parmelee. They
were a very nice family and we enjoyed the summers when the kids
were home from school. Leona was a sickly lady with severe heart
problems. We kids were very impressed by the housework and
cooking (like making bread) that these kids could do and how much
their mother taught them in her quiet way.

I remember Bill saying that he told his kids if they would make
the best of going to school at the government boarding school
that he would do his best to see that they all went to college.
And they did.

These letters from Bill were written during WWII and the Korean
War. I think they are the most descriptive and interesting of
the War letters we have. Bill was active in the American Legion
and always organized the patriotic observation of Memorial Day,
Independence Day and Veteran's Day.

Bill Hauff was a wise and inspiring man and I am glad that he was
part of my young life. As you will note from the letters he and
Dad shared a patriotic and politial connection.

4

Somewhere in England
17ᵗʰ of Ireland '44 (March)
(St. Patricks Day)

Dear Perry and all:,

Seems quite a while since I've last written, but always business before pleasure.

I hope you folks are all getting along OK and well, been wondering how you've been feeling since your operations and do hope you are much better as a result.

Have heard you've had immense amount of snow and cold weather this winter, must be sort of hard on the snow machinery of the High way dept. maybe of course too that those storms reported didn't effect Dak. as usualy.

Elvin has written from Australia but have lost track of all the other boys, perhaps over in this neck of the woods, haven't bumped into any, suppose we would have quite an army of our own once we get them into one outfit.

Getting along about election time again and suppose Sharpe and the others in the lead. don't know much about what has taken place along those line's at home, a person plays a different kind of game here, but retains a lot of its features like the old post trader and such with plenty of swapping, anyway when the cats away the mice will play, so we can't do much about it, there's going to be a time coming again. I've often wondered just how a lot of the scores will be settled when pay day arrives.

I'm getting along well enough, plenty of room for improvement, with 'casey to bat should bring results before long.

Would like to write of things im doing places and such we see but sure if in taboo list yet. We have weather here, now I like weather but this is sort of hard to stomach so much lower and different than desert, well if we stick around long enough guess I will.

Fortitude and a good stomach helps us along with the food, plenty good, even had an egg looking up for breakfast once.

Seems a definite shortage of good reading material even the funnys look darn good so send me one once in a while. Hope this will find you folks all well and do write occasionally,

most sincerely
Bill

9th Fox Hole on the right.
Somewhere in Holland
8th Oct 44

Dear Perry & all the Greeks:-

Seems like it's been a long time since have heard from any of you was wondering how you all are getting along and how's the pheasant hunting this year in the Dakotas. Has been a long time since tasted any and after a long period of what we do get a change, well we could stood it.

Again comes election time, suppose you fellers are at it hot & heavy, well lets keep those principles above the belt and have less personalities, of course, here we get frequent lessons in tolerations that are always overlooked in the land of plenty, too much!

Winter must be coming, heard some cranes & storks beating it South, maybe the racket of all the War paraphenalia scares 'em out, but we can feel those cold breezes, go right thru. It hasn't frosted here, the flowers are blooming, whats left of 'em, but the leaves of some trees are turning red and yellow and dropping on the ground. Sure would be nice to get this all over with before winter, then we wouldn't have to crawl in & out of these holes, makes me feel like a Coyote and its darn damp, not too far from water, but we either dig in or it hurts. Last July I bet a fellow off a pair of pink pants, this should be over with by Armistice day, well I'm commencing to feel those pink pants slipping figured I was betting on a cinch too, but its like a crop in Todd Co. Me thinks better we stay by the horses & cattle.

How are all the boys getting along, suppose most of them are in this T/O but I haven't run into any of them, yet.

The family seems to be getting along at home, but guess would be better if "Dad" was around, although there isn't much more could do for them. Luella writes, she hasn't seen me for almost a year and wants me home for Xmas, by the looks of things guess will be lucky if I can get away and home next year.

This is quite the country, everything has been kept so nice & clean, they have such swell farmsteads, reminds me so much of our Lakeview folks, go at things in a big way, those big windmills are really nice affairs, make darn good O.P.'s but Jerry usually knows that too & steels the stuffing out of them, they are quite modern in their homes & equipment but you can't help but notice the four years of Jerry occupation. Since we moved in it sure raises hell with the landscape. The traditional wooden shoes are much in evidence, & a good thing they are, so much rain & dampness, leather shoes rot and wear out fast in the sand & gravel.

There are many things wanted to bring out but guess with the shortage of paper, shall have to confine my remarks to the space available. Mr. Bose writes me occasionally, can predict his reelection, gee! I'm sunk.

Lets hear from you folks, see what's going on at the home front, since being air-borne, there is much less can tell you, but its mighty interesting, anyway regardless of the roughness involved, it's better than 6 hair-borne, for we do get many top-side views of this old world.

My sincere regards to all and so hope this finds you all in the best of health.
Most sincerely
Bill

150

Somewhere in Belgium
21st Jan 1945.

Dear Breeks:-

Thank you very much for the nice
Xmas card and your best wishes, its
nice to know folks at home think of
us and write.

We had a very white xmas this year here
but it was miserable, all in all, we
didnt have much time to celebrate, being
on the front lines is not a very nice place.

Your boys are sure pretty much
scattered out over the world, its
difficult to imagine the differences involved.
There will be some tall story telling
when they all get to-gether again and I
sincerely hope with you that it will
be soon. Did any of them turn out to be
paratroopers, or am I the worst of the lot.
Sure glad to hear the boys are all well
and like myself just make the best of it.
under all circumstances, wherever we may be
Alvin must be due for the rotation soon. He wrote

to me from the Philippines, it must
be hot there, of course it hasent been
cold here only the weather has been miserable.
Fortunately we have a roof over our heads
in place of canvas.

In spite of the rough going, have
been keeping well and feel fine
but tire easily. Have plenty of work
to keep one out of mischief.

Had one of my jeeps knocked
out in the past fracas but already
have a replacement so we won't have
to walk much we hope.

From the reports you must be having
a very cold spell of weather at home, well
just "keep those home fires burning", the
war certainly can't keep going forever and
of course we all want to ~~get~~ home as
soon as possible, the "furriners" are OK
but home's best

My kindest regards and best wishes
to all of you   Most Sincerely
                            Bill

Somewhere in Germany
13th Feb 1945

Dear Mr. & Mrs. Greek:

Thank you ever so much for writing me such interesting letters and the election returns were also the best I've had an opportunity of looking at. You wrote me on Nov. 11th and it came in to-day, and air mail at that, Crijes I'm wondering what it be like if you'd sent it regular mail, a classic example of efficiency no doubt, nevertheless was very glad to hear from the old stomping ground.

Believe I last wrote you from a damn fox hole in Holland and from France was able to send a Xmas card. We had to run the sonsabitches out of Belgium again and now see where it got me. Jumping around all over Europe, and brother, although I hate to admit it I'se getting three damn tired and am beginning to wonder

when they are "going to" holler enough.
Last heard from Billie, he wrote X-mas
Day, was in the States yet. He is
on an LST too like Shorty, don't
know what doing but they gave him
a course in Radio at the H. of Wise.
and he got a RM 3/c rating whatever
that means. From my experience the
ratings don't mean a hell of a lot,
considering what they handed Elvin & others

Henry must have taken the Instrument
& survey school at Roberts. in Artillery
That's what I had, and from what you
say same thing. only I had to
take Cav. OCS after I was trained in
Arty. Hope by now Elvin has had
the chance of getting home, deserves it.
Guess I'll have to stick out a while
yet. won't even have a chance to be home
to cash my bonds from the last war
coming due June 1st. just T/s I guess

I'm hoping your other boys Hank,
Lester & Dan are ok. If they come this way

send me their address I may be
able to look them up".

Tell Speny's hello for me and
to keep chins up.

Was sure glad to hear you are
getting along so well Perry, sure
dreaded to see you in that old hospital
but guess comes a time in life when
we have to get the old works repaired.
Better take it easy on the work, let
someone else get the hell jarred out
of em on that Blade. I remember
the boy who was in that room with
you at Omaha. Was sure sorry had
to move along so quick then & can
well imagine you are being kept
plenty busy now. Too many people
seem to ignore politics entirely,
in this day and age can't be did.
It's my belief that all this crap
we have to put up with now has been
caused by people not accepting the responsibility
of full citizenship, only yelling for handouts.

Been rougher'en a cob in these parts, had snow up to the belly button, and since the thaw, bottomless roads, with tanks & heavy traffic hammering the hell out of it & we have spring & summer to look forward to at least warmer weather. I've been froze up since the middle of Dec. and a dam old snow bank isn't so hot to sleep in. Jal got rushed out, before I had a chance to get winterized, and no anti-freeze much for my system.

Well, I will have to run along now, "Germany calling" to see if I can't find me a pill box the boys haven't blowed to hell, for some shelter to-nite, will probaly wind up sleeping in a lousy slit trench somewhere.

My regards to all our friends. I shall answer Caroline's letter later. Thanks again for writing, can't you do it more often? and dz excuse my English it stinks. Cheerio, Bill

Military Medals, Decorations, and Citations awarded to William A. Hauff

WWI Army of Occupation Medal.

Presented to United States military who served in the European occupation in WWI. A likeness of General John J. Pershing is on the medal.

WWI Victory Medal with Meuse-Argonne Battle Clasp and One Bronze Star.

The Bronze Star was awarded to soldiers cited for gallantry in action between 1917 and 1920. The clasp, inscribed with the Meuse-Argonne Battle, denotes participation in the major ground conflict, the largest and bloodiest battle in American history when a series of Allied attacks known as the Hundred Days Offensive brought an end to the war. The battle cost 26,277 American lives, 28,000 German lives, and undocumented French lives.

Basic Combat Parachutist Badge.

Awarded after completing a three-phase course of ground phase, tower phase, and jump phase, which included a no-load jump and progressed to a full combat load jump at night.

Combat Glider Badge.

Honoring his participation in at least one combat glider mission into enemy-held territory.

Combat Infantryman Badge.

 Awarded to infantrymen and Special Forces soldiers in the rank of Colonel or below who fought in active ground combat. It recognizes the infantrymen who continuously operated under the worst conditions while performing a mission not assigned to any other Soldier or unit. A recipient must have been personally present and under hostile fire.

WWII American Campaign Medal.

Recognized the military members who performed military service in the American Theater of Operations during WWII.

WWII European-African-Middle Eastern Campaign Medal with Four Bronze Stars.

The EAME was first awarded to General Dwight Eisenhower for his service as Supreme Commander of the Allied Expeditionary Force during WWII. The medal was presented to service members who participated in one or more designated military campaigns.

Bronze Star.

Awarded to Master Sergeant William A. Hauff on February 4, 1944, for exemplary conduct while serving in the 508th Parachute Infantry Regiment in ground combat in the battle known as D-Day.

Presidential Unit Citation.

Awarded to units of armed services for extraordinary heroism between December 7, 1941, the attack on Pearl Harbor, and the start of American involvement in WWII. The awarded unit must have displayed such gallantry, determination, and esprit de corps in accomplishing its mission under extremely difficult and hazardous conditions so as to set the unit apart from and above other units in the same campaign.

WWII Victory Medal.

Awarded to members of the U.S. military who served on active duty or as reservists between December 7, 1941, and December 31, 1946.

WWII Army of Occupation Medal with Japan Clasp.

To be awarded, a service member must have performed at least 30 consecutive days of military duty within a designated area of military occupation.

National Defense Service Medal (Korea).

Awarded to service members who served honorably from June 27, 1950, to July 27, 1954, during the declaration of a national emergency of the Korean War.

PHILADELPHIA ...

THIS IS A REQUISITION FOR MEDAL OR MEDALS AS INDICATED IN THIS LETTER. ENGRAVING SHOULD BE DONE AS REQUIRED AND MEDAL OR MEDALS SHIPPED TO THE ADDRESSEE INDICATED.

IN REPLY REFER TO
AGPD-C 201 Hauff, William A.
(23 Apr 48) RA 37 250 377

COPY

1[illegible] June 1948

SUBJECT: Letter Orders

THRU:

TO: Master Sergeant William A. Hauff, RA 37 250 377

1. By direction of the President, under the provisions of Executive Order 9419, 4 February 1944, (Sec. II, WD Bul. 3, 1944), a Bronze Star Medal is awarded to Master Sergeant (then Second Lieutenant) William A. Hauff, RA 37 250 377, 508th Parachute Infantry Regiment, for exemplary conduct in ground combat against the armed enemy on or about 6 June 1944 in the European Theater of Operations.

2. Authority for this award is contained in Par. 15.1c AR 600-45, and is based upon General Orders No. 50, Headquarters 508th Parachute Infantry Regiment dated 11 August 1944.

3. The Commanding Officer, Philadelphia Quartermaster Depot, will forward an engraved Bronze Star Medal direct to the recipient at the address shown above.

BY ORDER OF THE SECRETARY OF THE ARMY:

1 Incl
BSM Certificate

Adjutant General

588899

REQUISITION TO PHILADELPHIA QM DEPOT

0718

PREVIOUS EDITION MAY BE USED

Letter to Master Sergeant William A. Hauff notifying him of his award of the Bronze Star Medal.

During my research, I discovered the significance of the four bronze service stars that Hauff received with his WWII European-African-Middle East Campaign Medal. A star was awarded for each campaign he participated in—Normandy, Rhineland, Ardennes-Alsace, and Central Europe. These four battles, milestones in the war, occurred within nine months. Only a small percentage of WWII soldiers were awarded four stars.

The Normandy star was for D-Day when the 508th PIR jumped pre-dawn under heavy cloud coverage behind well-fortified enemy lines, among the first Allied soldiers to cripple Hitler's increasing invasion of France.

The Rhineland star was awarded for the 508th PIR daytime combat jump fifty-three miles behind enemy lines, where the 508th captured strategic ground. This jump was the first battle on German soil.

The Ardennes-Alsace star was for engaging in heavy combat with the German army, pushing them out of Belgium and back to Germany. Coined "The Battle of the Bulge" by Churchill, it was a German counteroffensive in the rugged wooded country of the Ardennes. Fighting began in December 1944 and continued through January 1945. Losing almost half of his army—an estimated 120,000 men—Hitler's advances to overpower the Allied coalition failed. Hauff's letter, "Somewhere in Belgium," was written during this historic retreat of the German army. He writes: "We had a very white Christmas this year here, but it was miserable, all in all, we didn't have much time to celebrate, being on the front lines is not a very nice place." The winter of 1944 – 1945 was one of the coldest winters on record in Belgium. Hauff, now permanently assigned to the 82nd Airborne, met up with the 7th Armored Division on December 20, 1944.

The Central Europe star was awarded for participating in the Western Allied invasion of Nazi Germany in the final months of World War II from March 22, 1945 – May 11, 1945.

Adolf Hitler committed suicide on April 30, 1945.

The Germans surrendered on May 8, 1945.

Japan surrendered on September 2, 1945.

William A. Hauff remained in active service until the very end of the war.

In 1946-1947, before the Korean War started, Hauff was stationed in Taejon, Korea, when he learned of the passing of his wife, Leona.

Leona Mattie (Brown) Hauff
November 22, 1903 – March 11, 1947

William wrote to the Greek family from Young Dong, Korea, on June 24, 1947, reflecting on the change in the children's lives and how he needed to get home to them.

"Have decided now that things have calmed down a bit, to get back and steer those youngsters of mine a little, try to keep them on an even keel, the boys will get along alright, and Luella needs to have her daddy with her a few more years, about all I can do for her. Maybe if conditions will permit, I thought of getting her enrolled along with Sylvan at Pine Ridge, who has two more years there yet, she may get along alright there."

William remarried in 1948 to Golda (Cowell) Brown, the widow of Harold Brown. Harold was no relation to the Joseph Brown family of this book, but his mother's name was coincidentally Leona Brown. The couple were married for two years when Golda was diagnosed with cancer and succumbed to the disease in 1951. My dad never spoke of this second marriage. I heard about it for the first time from a cousin when I was in my 50s. When I asked my dad about it, he confirmed it was true. William and Golda moved to Kansas so she could be near her oncologist, and William spent all of his savings on her medical care. My dad went to Kansas to live with them the summer he graduated from Oglala Community High School before he entered the army. He would not comment on his time in Kansas or specifics regarding Golda. His body language told me that he was still not happy with his dad's second marriage, yet he would not criticize either of them.

As a civilian, William served as the Bennett County Auditor/Treasurer from 1953 until his death in 1963.

The William A. Hauff family. L to R: Sylvan, Billie, William, Leona, Luella, and Dick.

Dear Friends,

The coming election on November 4th will again permit each of you to exercise the American privilege of casting your ballot for the candidate of your choice. My name appears on that ballot in the Republican column as I am seeking to serve you in the office of County Auditor. Because it will be impossible for me to contact all of you personally before election time, I am using this means to ask you for your vote and support in the coming election.

I submit to you the following as a statement of my qualifications:

1. I have been a lifelong resident of the immediate areas.

2. I have been a resident and taxpayer of Bennett County for the past six years.

3. I am a veteran of three wars and a good share of my work in the service was connected with administrative affairs. This work has been somewhat along the line that will be performed in the office of County Auditor and I feel that the experience I've gained in the service and other positions of trust and responsibility I've held in my lifetime qualifies me for that post.

I promise that if I am elected I shall devote all my time and do my best to operate the office of County Auditor in a competent, cooperative and completely impartial manner, affording to all citizens of Bennett County, insofar as I am able, efficient and economical service.

Thanking you in advance for your vote and support.

Sincerely yours,

William (Bill) A. Hauff

Dick, Sylvan, Luella, and Billie at their father's funeral. Martin, South Dakota 1963.

SYLVAN AND MARGARET (SKALINDER) HAUFF

Sylvan Hauff, age 1

Margaret, on the right, age 11, on the Skalinder ranch.
The older sister, Mary Ann, is on the left, with their family friend, Joe Condoleezza.

Sylvan, age 2, feeds chickens on the Hauff ranch.
"My first job," he said.

Luella and Sylvan Hauff

Dick, Luella, and Sylvan Hauff

Teen Years

Sylvan with BB Gun at Hauff house in Rapid City.

Sylvan's first selfie BEFORE cell phones c. 1947.

Margaret, center in a polka dot dress. 8th grade,
St. Mary's School for Indian Girls,
Springfield, SD. c. 1944.

Margaret is on the left with her friend, Jacque McCue

Margaret, Homecoming Queen (standing in the center.) Bennett County High School. 1947/1948.

Margaret at a family branding. c. 1949

Sylvan's senior picture, 1949.

Margaret's senior picture, 1948.

JACK D RUNNELS

PEARL BISSONETTE

LEROY A BAD WOUND

JEANNIE MAE GILLESPIE

MANUEL C MORAN

BOBBY BREWER

JEANETTE F RANDALL

ETHELYN JACOBS
TREASURER

LAVERN H LITTLE HAWK

SYLVAN HAUFF
PRESIDENT

MRS EVELYN BERGEN
SPONSOR

MARION JANIS
VICE-PRESIDENT

MR CLIFFORD W KING
PRINCIPAL

REBECCA IRON HAWK
SECRETARY

BILLY BREWER

JOHN C BRIGGS YELLOW

CLAUDIA IRON HAWK

1949

O.C.H.S. SENIORS

O'Neill Photo Co.

Sylvan Hauff, Senior Class President at Oglala Community High School.

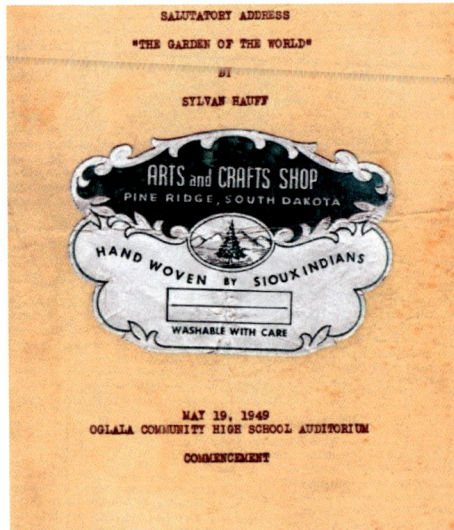

SALUTATORY ADDRESS

"THE GARDEN OF THE WORLD"

BY

SYLVAN HAUFF

ARTS and CRAFTS SHOP
PINE RIDGE, SOUTH DAKOTA

HAND WOVEN BY SIOUX INDIANS

WASHABLE WITH CARE

MAY 19, 1949
OGLALA COMMUNITY HIGH SCHOOL AUDITORIUM

COMMENCEMENT

COMMENCEMENT

Thursday, May 19, 1949   8:00 P.M.

OCHS Auditorium

Part 1
THE KEYS OF LIFE
(A pageant written and directed by the senior class and sponsor.)

Readers:. . . . . Lavern Little Hawk and Manuel Moran

Scene I. Health. . . . . . Written by Pearl Bissonette, Jeanette Randall

Scene II Worthy Home Membership...Written by Marion Janis, Ethelyn Jacobs

Scene III. Vocational Guidance..Written by Lavern Little Hawk, Bobby Brewer

Scene IV. Good Citizenship.Written by Leroy Bad Wound, Jennie Mae Gillespie

Scene V   Command of Fundmental Tools.Written by Sylvan Hauff, Billy Brewer

Scene VI Worthy Use of Leisure. . . . . Written by Manuel Moran

Scene VII Ethical Character. . . .Written by Claudia and Rebecca Iron Hawk

Symbolic Interlude:. . . . . Peace Pipe Ceremony
Chief Spotted Crow - - -Senior Class
Part 11.

Salutatory. . . . . Sylvan Hauff

Valedictory. . . . . .Rebecca Iron Hawk

Presentation of class. . . . . .Mr. Clifford King

Presentation of diplomas. . . . . Mr. Albert T. Pyles

Song. . . . . Senior Double Quartette

Presentation of the peace pipe. . . . . Sylvan Hauff

Acceptance of the peace pipe. . . . . . . Morris Eagle Elk, Jr. President

Processional. . . . . Mrs. Evelyn L. Bergen

Sylvan Hauff, Salutatorian for Oglala Community High School Graduation, 1949

The garden of the world is a paradise of miracles and wonders, and only those who have their inner sights set and can see the infinite mysteries of life may hope to recognize it. In every tiny seed lies the eternal glory of creation; in every blossom the promise of greater possibilities, of which the fruit is the perfect fulfillment.

Tonight, we, as a class, are pushing out from the tiny seed to grow upward into the expression of maturer life. In years past, we have been sheltered in the tiny sphere of the seedling, protected by the shell of youth from the rougher elements of the soil. For several years, we few human seedlings have been nourished in this one fertile spot in the universal garden; our Gardeners have been those who first saw within the rude husks, the inner value that was concealed from any but the understanding eye. Now comes the Spring-time call of life's eternal change. Now we must put forth individual stalks of vigorous, useful planthood. It has been a safe, happy season of growth to us-- this period of our high school germination--wherein we have grown side by side and felt ourselves very close of kin. It is a thought of no little sadness, that from this hour of our sprouting outward, we will grow apart in all our thoughts, feelings, and desires, and each becomes transplanted to his own natural habitat, and takes root in the soil to which his own tastes and possibilities must essentially assign him.

This then is the hour of our transplanting. We must test in other soils, the theories we have gatherd during our, all too brief, germination period.

Dear friends, my classmates have conferred upon me the great honor of speaking the words that shall bid you welcome here tonight. I am greatful to them for this mark of their favor, but still, as I look around upon your faces so clearly marked with the lines of wisdom and greater experience, I cannot but feel that the words of welcome should come from you. It is we who are passing into your midst, we who are joining you in the larger school of progress outside these doors.

Then, while we do truely thank you most humbly for coming, and trust you may have every cause to long remember the associations of this hour, yet we feel that we must also ask your forebearance and kindly sympathy, and crave from each of you, as we step forth into your midst, the warm handshake and cordial that will assure us of your joy at bidding us welcome.

Sylvan's Salutatory Speech at Graduation
Even then, he was thinking about gardening.

Four months after graduating from high school, Sylvan attended his first year at the University of South Dakota in Vermillion, majoring in Social Work with minors in German, Psychology, and Government. He told me it was a tough year with no time to make friends. He was still grieving the loss of his mother and wished he could have had her loving, reassuring advice during this transition. He never forgot her telling him she wanted him to go to college.

OCHS did not have an advanced course curriculum to prepare students for a four-year university, and although he was at the top of his high school class, he was ill-prepared for college-level courses. His freshman-year grades at the University were poor, and he said it was a humbling experience. He studied all night, attended classes all day, and was required to be active in the Reserve Officers' Training Corp (ROTC), which demanded a lot of time and energy.

In his sophomore year, he raised his grades to A's and B's "with an occasional C" and began to enjoy college life. He received his Bachelor of Arts degree on June 1, 1953.

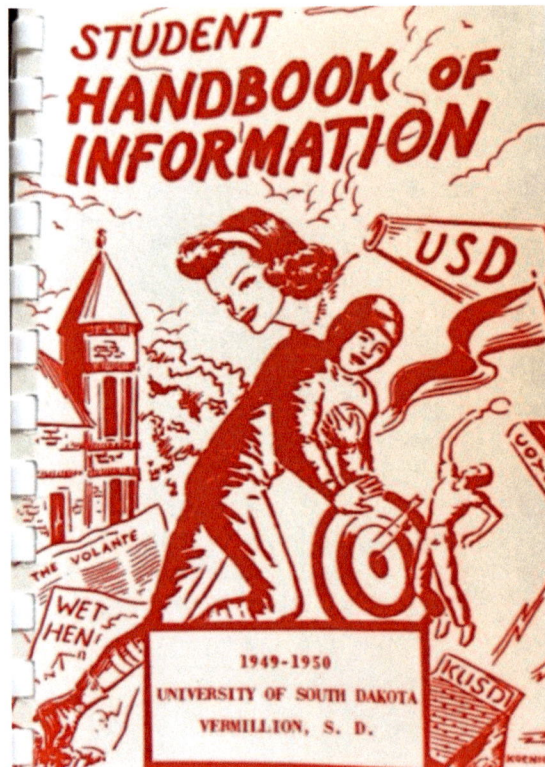

After graduation, he went into the military to fulfill his obligation to serve two years as required by the U.S. Army ROTC scholarship program, which funded his college education. During his four years at the University, he earned the rank of Second Lieutenant, and in July 1953, he reported to Ft. Benning, Georgia, to complete Officer Training. After Ft. Benning, he was stationed as the Infantry Unit Commander at Ft. Leonard Wood, MO. His next stop was Germany during the Korean War, where he was assigned to the 6th Armored Division.

Takes Officers Training

LT. SYLVAN R. HAUFF
Lt. Sylvan R. Hauff of the

He was awarded the highest qualification for the Army Rifle Expert Marksmanship Medal, the National Defense Service Medal during the Korean War, and an Army of Occupation Medal-Germany. On June 7, 1955, under President Eisenhower, he was promoted to the Reserve Commissioned Officer grade of First Lieutenant. His active-duty discharge went into effect on August 16, 1955, and he served in the Army Reserve until his honorable discharge in 1963.

Sylvan did not share the same enthusiasm for the military with his father. As a child raised in a government boarding school that offered no privacy, required to march to meals and classes, wear a uniform, and follow a strict schedule under authoritarian rule, he was anxious to be done with a regimented life.

In the summer of 1955, having completed his two-year stint of active duty for the Army, he went to Martin, South Dakota, to visit his father. It was here he reconnected with his childhood sweetheart, my mother, Margaret Skalinder Ward. Mom had divorced my biological father, Gerald Ward, immediately after I was born. For the first year and a half of my life, I lived in the Skalinder home in Martin with my grandparents Arthur and Zona, mother, sister April, and brother Steve. In December 1955, my mother became Mrs.

Sylvan Hauff, and we moved to Winner, South Dakota. Sylvan had a ready-made family and accepted the responsibility with generosity, kindness, and love. In 1956, he petitioned the court for the adoption of Margaret's three children, and it was finalized on January 15, 1957. April had just turned seven, Steven was three, and I was two. Sylvan was the only father I ever knew, and I have been forever grateful that my mom accepted his marriage proposal.

Ready-made family. Margaret, Tracy, Steven, and April.

Sylvan Hauff, Commissioned Officer

First Lieutenant Hauff

During the three months of their short engagement, Sylvan wrote a love letter to Margaret every evening when he returned home from his job as a Social Worker for the Department of Public Welfare in Winner, South Dakota. He forgot to write a letter to her one night and apologized profusely. The German salutation "Meine liebling" translates to "my darling." I am not sure what Desi' meant. Possibly a nickname he had for her.

Winner, South Dakota
October 26, 1955
Wednesday night 8:45

Meine liebling Desi',

As usually is the case these days, I have been thinking of you almost continuously all day today, and I have been looking forward to this evening when I would be able to write to you again. I am sorry Darling, that I must begin this letter with an apology for my neglect last night, when I should have written to you but I did not because I did not get home until a very late hour and did not feel very well either. But I really should have written if I had not been so lazy, and in the future I shall let nothing interfere with my correspondence with you.

The following letter is one of my favorites, as Dad mentions the picture Mom gave him when they were children. This photo is shown in Part Two, Page 50.

Winner, South Dakota
October 31, 1955
Halloween Night

My beloved and bewitching Margaret,

How is my favorite goblin tonight? I hope you realize that you are the one ghost with whom I would like to prowl the countryside tonight, and that I am feeling very lonely right now because I cannot be with you as

I was so fortunate to be last night. So, I shall do the one thing which will provide some satisfaction, write to you and tell you how much I love you. Your picture is standing on the table in front of me and I can look at it while I write. Did I neglect to thank you for picture, Darling? You will never be able to guess how much I appreciate having a picture of you, since, as you may recall, you never provided me with one before except for the little photograph which I received from you so many years ago and which I have always kept very fondly. You were just a little girl when the picture was made, and perhaps a trifle skinny at the time, but I can still remember the thrill of receiving the picture and part of that same feeling comes back to me still, whenever I look at it.

It is strange and mysterious how things have worked out for us, isn't it Darling? Before long, you shall discover that I have a primitive side to me that causes me to think in terms of "magic" or at least Supernaturalism, when actually no one realizes more clearly than I that there must be a more reliable explanation for things than to attribute them to some supernatural being. This is not to say that I do not believe that divine providence does guide the development of people, but usually what appears to be the work of angels can be explained in scientific terms. Whether or not we are justified in doing this is of course a question in theology, and although I know nothing of it, I sometimes think about it and wonder how it will all turn out in the end. In the meantime, when I can find no logical scientific explanation for something, I find myself more or less subconsciously assigning its cause to that mysterious realm about which we know nothing. I do not consider this abnormal, do you? After all, it has not been so many years ago that people were being burned at the stake for being "witches." Anyway, it is interesting to consider this sort of thing, and perhaps particularly apropos tonight, since this is the time when Science is thrown out the window and witches ride their brooms across the sky as they used to when I was a little boy.

In the letter below, he tells Margaret about a typical workday that really is anything but.

Winner, South Dakota
November 3, 1955
Thursday night 8:00

Dear Princess,

We had a very busy day at the office today, and I visited the jail and several other places around town in connection with some cases. This afternoon I visited an old man who lives in town in an old shack and is a bachelor. The poor old fellow is in very bad shape, but he will not consider moving into an Old People's Home. He had greatly swollen ankles and the circulation in these extremities was so poor that the skin had broken open on each leg. He had not had any medical attention for these lesions, and they looked terrible. I immediately contacted the city health officer to see if some treatment could be secured right away. I found the doctor's office so crowded that I could hardly get in the door, so, after consulting with him and getting some medicine to reduce the swelling and improve circulation, I stopped at the Drug Store and got some ointment and bandages and returned to the old fellow's house, where I treated the wounds for him and bandaged them securely. I think he will get along better now, but I will stop and check on him again in a day or two to make sure he bathes the legs with the boric acid which I left for him and treats them again. Vern and I are going to try to convince him of the advantages of moving into one of the homes here in town, but I know it will take some work on our part. He is such a pleasant fellow in spite of his many afflictions, and one cannot help but like him. I find that there is much misunderstanding concerning older people and that they are not usually appreciated nearly as much as they should be. This is unfortunate because older people need to be understood and helped as much as anyone else. Some of the old people I visit each day are so happy to be able to visit and discuss their problems with someone, and one is impressed by the need which is so evident here.

Sylvan got employment with the Federal Government in 1957, and the family moved from Winner to Sioux Falls. Four more children were born there—Echo, Alison, Brad, and Brian. Sylvan worked for the federal government for the next 28 years, retiring in 1984 as Chief Federal Probation Officer for the State of South Dakota, the highest level of achievement in his field. He was only fifty-five, but it was the mandatory retirement age per Federal Law Enforcement Hazardous Duty provisions. In his honor, a flag was flown over the United States Capitol building in Washington, D.C., and November 29, 1984, was proclaimed Sylvan R. Hauff Day in the State of South Dakota.

After cultivating and harvesting grapes to make Pennington County Fair prize-winning wine, trying his hand at woodworking and his feet at ballroom dancing, birdwatching, and reading, reading, reading, he received a call from Lynn, Jackson, Shultz, Lebrun, P.C. Attorneys at Law. They wanted him to work for their firm as a private investigator. He accepted and soon found himself once again navigating the dusty, unmarked back roads on the Pine Ridge Indian Reservation. In the mid-1990s, after working for over forty years, he retired for good to enjoy his many hobbies and eight grandchildren.

When Margaret was 68, she surprised the family by enrolling in a four-year Theology program. She and Dad were devout members of the Episcopalian Church, and her grandfather, Peter Skalinder, had been a lay reader at Grace Episcopal Church in LaCreek, South Dakota. Reverend Vine Deloria was a close family friend who visited them often while she was growing up. She had been mentored in her faith since childhood, and deciding to become a late-in-life theology student meant a lot to her. She dedicated the next four years to nightly studies, graduating from the School of Theology University of the South in 1998 with a degree in Education for Ministry. She was 72, and we were all so proud of her.

Sylvan harvesting his grapes.

Chokecherry wine made from berries picked on the Hauff family land in Porcupine, SD, on the Pine Ridge Reservation.

Handyman Hauff

PROBATION SYSTEM
UNITED STATES COURTS

This certifies that

Sylvan R. Hauff

the United States Probation Officer identified in this credential by photograph and signature is the official representative of the United States Courts and the United States Department of Justice in the performance of his duties in connection with probation and parole.

Issued at Washington, D. C.   August 3, 1959

Warren Olney III
Director, Administrative Office
of the United States Courts

United States Probation Officer

FEDERAL PROBATION
OFFICERS ASSOCIATION

Sylvan R. Hauff

IS A MEMBER IN GOOD STANDING FOR
THE YEAR ENDING DEC. 31, 1965

233   SECRETARY-TREASURER

SYLVAN R. HAUFF
SUPERVISING PROBATION OFFICER
U. S. DISTRICT COURT
DISTRICT OF SOUTH DAKOTA

OFFICE: 342-4240   515 NINTH STREET
RM. 257 FEDERAL BLDG   RAPID CITY, S. D. 57701

United States Courts

SYLVAN R. HAUFF
Chief Probation and Parole Officer

Rm. 257, Federal Building   U.S. District Court
515 9th Street   District Of South Dakota
Rapid City, SD 57701   (605) 342-4240

WINNER ADVOCATE

AND TRIPP COUNTY JOURNAL

WINNER, SOUTH DAKOTA, THURSDAY, AUGUST 4, 1966

Section 2

Page 1

Sioux Descendent Has Very Special Mission: He Works to Rebuild Shattered Lives of Men

(Following is another in a series of articles on prominent Indian citizens of South Dakota. The series, carried weekly in the WINNER ADVOCATE, is a project of the Winner Lions Club, which is carrying it out with the special assistance of Harold Schunk, superintendent of the Rosebud Reservation.)

Sylvan R. Hauff of Sioux Falls has a special mission in life.

He helps to rebuild shattered lives.

Hauff, who is of Sioux lineage, is a probation officer for the United State's district court in Sioux Falls.

A professional social worker with a special interest in the rehabilitation of juvenile and youthful offenders, this week indicated his belief that far too often the accomplishments of distinguished Sioux Indians of South Dakota go unnoticed.

"Successful members of this cultural group," believes Hauff, "have gone unnoticed and unrecognized, while those at the opposite end of the social spectrum have too often been accepted as the "typical Indian'."

"Social ostracism" based upon "racial or cultural misconceptions" are "neither understandable or commendable," believes Hauff.

Hauff, who is one-quarter Sioux, was graduated from high school in Pine Ridge in 1949. A standout football player in his high school years, he was salutatorian of his graduating class and a representative of his school at Boy's State.

Following high school he enrolled at the University of South Dakota at Vermillion, where he majored in social work and minored in psychology, German and government. While in college he earned a reserve commission as a second lieutenant in the U.S. Army, accomplishing this through an ROTC program.

After his graduation from college in June of 1953 he was called to active duty with the army and was given a command of an infantry company at Ft. Leonard Wood, Mo.

He was sent to West Germany, where he was promoted to First Lieutenant.

After his discharge from the army in 1955, he accepted a job as social caseworker with the Department of Public Welfare n Winner.

While in Winner he acquired valuable experience as a social worker and also a wife.

On December 17, 1956, he was named a federal probation officer for the District of South Dakota.

From Winner he moved to Sioux Falls, where he has made his home since.

There is a need, believes Hauff, for "additional basic research" into the causes of social ills. And these needs, he warns, "are becoming more critical with our burgeoning population."

Hauff is married and the father of seven children.

Hauff promoted to supervising probation officer

Sylvan R. Hauff, Rapid City, has been appointed supervising U.S. probation officer for the district of South Dakota.

Hauff received the appointment this month from U.S. District Judge Fred J. Nichol, after more than 20 years of service.

His new duties will include supervision and training of recently appointed probation officers and overseeing the work of Probation Officer Assistant Ernest Little White Man of Kyle.

Hauff has lived in Rapid City since 1970 when he left the federal probation office in Sioux Falls.

Rapid City man named chief probation officer

Sylvan R. Hauff of Rapid City has been named the chief U.S. probation officer for South Dakota effective April 1.

Hauff, a 25-year veteran of the federal probation service, was appointed by U.S. District Judge Andrew Bogue. He was born at Rosebud and is a member of the Oglala Sioux Tribe.

He entered the probation service in Sioux Falls in 1956 and was transferred to Rapid City in 1970 when a U.S. District Court was established here. He was promoted to supervising U.S. probation officer six years later.

The former Army officer and social worker succeeds Charles B. Mandsager of Sioux Falls. Probation agency headquarters will be moved to Rapid City.

The probation service is responsible for conducting investigations for the courts and supervising persons out on probation or parole. It has nine probation officers, two paraprofessional workers and six clerical employees with offices in Rapid City, Sioux Falls, Pierre, Mission and Kyle.

Top probation officer in state retires

Ken Baka
Staff Writer

Sylvan Hauff has seen many changes in the federal criminal justice system during his 28 years as a probation officer, but nothing as great as the changes coming after his retirement.

Hauff, the federal government's top probation officer in South Dakota, retired Friday, just six weeks after Congress passed the Comprehensive Crime Control Act of 1984, a major get-tough piece of legislation.

The act — so comprehensive that it covers offenses committed on the moon — means major changes in federal probation offices throughout the nation, as well as for federal judges and prosecutors.

It also reverses a trend toward rehabilitation and re-emphasizes punishment of criminals and protection of society, Hauff said.

Hauff has been an advocate of rehabilitation and believes it could be successful. He has formed that opinion after years of supervising paroled convicts and probationers.

"It'll be interesting to see how all this will work out," said Hauff during an interview last week. "It'll be kind of an exciting time. I'm a little sorry I'm leaving."

In some of the biggest changes, the act:

Overhauls the Bail Reform Act of 1966 so that a defendant's danger to society must be considered when setting bond.

Eliminates a judge's sentencing discretion by setting up sentencing guidelines.

Replaces the old parole system with a program called "supervised release,"

in which judges maintain jurisdiction over criminals.

Restricts the insanity defense.

Makes it a federal crime to assault probation officer.

Adds sodomy and maiming to the 14 major crimes under federal jurisdiction on federal reservations.

Mandates a five-year sentence for people convicted of a federal offense while armed with a firearm.

Creates credit-card violations.

Increases court-appointed attorneys' fees.

Makes it a violation to leak information from government computers.

Hauff's is a forced retirement because the work of federal probation officers is classified as hazardous duty. By law, he must retire at age 55, which came Wednesday.

Hauff, a Rosebud native and graduate of the University of South Dakota, was named chief of the U.S. Probation Office in South Dakota in 1982. In the six years before then, he was second in command of the office's 16 probation officers.

In South Dakota, the Probation Office is based in Rapid City and has offices in Sioux Falls, Pierre, Mission and Kyle. The office comes under the authority of U.S. District Judge Andrew Bogue, who has not yet named Hauff's successor.

The Probation Office is a little-known arm of the the federal court system, known officially as Administrative Office of U.S. Courts.

Its officers are part sleuth, part police officer, part big brother. They probe a criminal's background for confidential information that a judge uses to hand down a sentence. They supervise the lifestyles of criminals who are

sentenced to probation instead of time behind bars. And they help prison parolees adjust to the outside world, where flirtation with the law risks being returned to prison.

Over the last year, the Rapid City office has supervised about 450 probationers and parolees in South Dakota.

Hauff became a probation officer in 1956 in Sioux Falls. Many of the ensuing 14 years there were spent traveling to West River and the various Indian reservations.

"I spent at least half my time on the road," he said, "and with all kinds of people."

He fondly recalls the time he was supervising the parole of six murderers at the same time. They were mature and punctual.

"It was really a pleasure to work for most of them and they never gave us nearly as much trouble as young guys, car thieves, and so forth."

Hauff, who carries a weapon, said a probation officer's work is "exciting" but has "very distinct hazards." He often must travel alone to remote areas of the state to snuff out parolees who can become hostile when he appears at their doors.

"We've dealt with millionaires and lots of paupers, the powerful and the weak," he said. He's forbidden to talk about specific criminals with whom he's worked, or discuss the government's guarded witness protection program, which gives criminals new identities and new locations in exchange for information.

A most difficult aspect of the job is to be able to form a trusting relationship with the probationer or parolee, and then know when to become authoritative with the threat of proba-

tion revocation. It's a balancing act of society's interests against the individual's.

"It's kind of a tricky thing to do to turn authority on and off," he said. "We deliberately try to avoid playing the role of the police officer."

He's found that most criminals have "personality problems" manifested in alcoholism, and have average educations, intelligence and health. He's also seen a gradual increase in the number of probationers and parolees since 1970, reflecting what he called a "breakdown of family, unemployment and drug and alcohol involvement." About half of the federal court's criminals end up on probation; probationers outnumber parolees in South Dakota 7 to 3, he said.

Hauff, an advocate of rehabilitation, said "by and large" confinement doesn't rehabilitate a criminal. If rehabilitation has not always succeeded, it's because probation offices haven't had the resources to accomplish their goals, he said.

If probation officers had the money that the government spends to confine people and could use that to help people cope with society and stay within the law, "it would be money well-spent," he said.

In retirement, Hauff said he'll miss working within the prestige of the court system and also with "the little people."

"I can't say I regretted associating with known criminals. I've been rewarded by it in subtle ways, I guess."

Hauff and his wife, Margaret, will "take it easy" and "see what's available." He enjoys gardening and woodworking. He'll be honored at a farewell party with federal court officials Thursday.

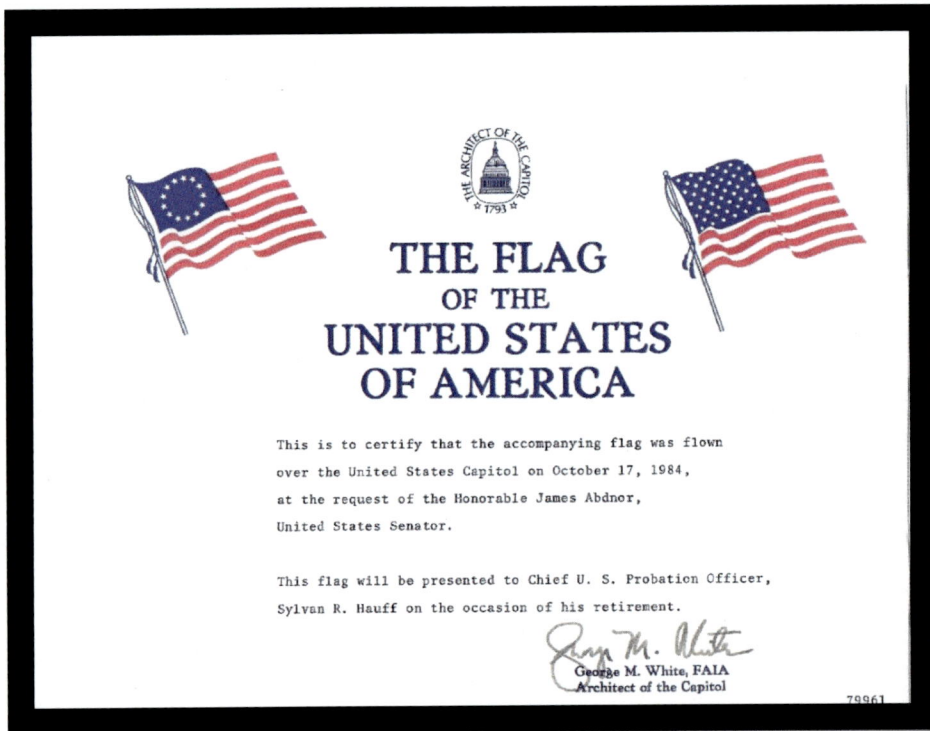

THE FLAG
OF THE
UNITED STATES
OF AMERICA

This is to certify that the accompanying flag was flown over the United States Capitol on October 17, 1984, at the request of the Honorable James Abdnor, United States Senator.

This flag will be presented to Chief U. S. Probation Officer, Sylvan R. Hauff on the occasion of his retirement.

George M. White, FAIA
Architect of the Capitol

79961

Executive Proclamation
State of South Dakota
Office Of The Governor

WHEREAS, Sylvan R. Hauff has been a faithful public servant of the United States of America for thirty years, twenty-eight of them with the Federal Probation Service; and,

WHEREAS, Sylvan began his career as a United States Probation Officer in Sioux Falls in December, 1956, was transferred to the Rapid City office in 1970 to establish and head a branch office, was designated Supervising Probation Officer in 1976, and became Chief Probation Officer in early 1982; and,

WHEREAS, Sylvan has been dedicated to his calling and has worked diligently and tirelessly for the betterment of the Federal Probation Service; and,

WHEREAS, Sylvan has helped literally thousands of offenders return as productive members of society, thus enriching the offenders and South Dakota as a whole; and,

WHEREAS, In Sylvan's honor, co-workers, friends and relatives will gather in the United States District Courtroom in Rapid City on November 29, 1984, to wish him a happy, well-deserved retirement and to revere his service to the people of this State and Nation:

NOW, THEREFORE, I, WILLIAM J. JANKLOW, Governor of the State of South Dakota, do hereby proclaim November 29, 1984, as

SYLVAN R. HAUFF DAY

in South Dakota, and I join his many friends in thanking Sylvan Hauff for all his many contributions through the years which have made South Dakota a better place in which to live and work.

IN WITNESS WHEREOF, I have hereunto set my hand and caused to be affixed the Great Seal of the State of South Dakota, in Pierre, the Capital City, this Twenty-Eighth Day of November, in the Year of Our Lord, Nineteen Hundred and Eighty-Four

WILLIAM J. JANKLOW, GOVERNOR

ATTEST:

Chambers of
Andrew W. Bogue
Chief Judge

318 Federal Building
Rapid City, South Dakota 57701

November 30, 1984

Mr. Sylvan Hauff
Chief U. S. Probation Officer
U. S. Probation Service
247 Federal Building
Rapid City, SD   57701

Dear Sylvan:

I just want to let you know in writing about the things that have been filling my mind leading up to your retirement. I do not know anything that has hit me this hard in a long time. We have had such a tremendous relationship with you and your office that the loss will be traumatic for me. Your expertise in your profession is widely recognized and admired. Your judgment has never let me down and I have to admit that I probably leaned on you too much. I am sure that it probably constituted a burden for you.

At any rate, Sylvan, you will be sorely missed and I wish you the best of everything in the future.

As a final note, I hope that I can talk you into doing some investigative work for the indigent defendants so that we can at least see that you are around the federal building part of the time.

Sincerely,

Andrew W. Bogue

AWB:jr

I contacted Judge Jane Wipf Pfeifle to ask her to say a few words about her time working with my dad. Below is the letter she wrote.

When I had the privilege of working with your dad, I recall him as being collegial, professional, and so intelligent. He had a terrific manner and was an excellent teacher. He taught me about important cultural practices and communication styles that I found helpful my whole career. I especially remember him describing how Lakota people maintained good relations with in-laws when they lived in close proximity: a husband would speak to his wife who would then relay that information to her mother, even if all were in the same room. He said this practice ensured that all were civil and kind to one another — essentially group harmony. He noted that the practice had continued to modern day even though people no longer lived in tipis where close quarters might otherwise provoke quarrels. He helped me understand that the term "Indian time," which I viewed as denigrating, could be understood as "we start when everyone is ready." We talked about how big the reservation is and how far people must travel, that it makes sense to wait, acknowledging that there were impediments to travel. He helped me understand that when someone didn't look me in the eye, it wasn't because they were not being truthful, but respectful. We discussed the strong cultural tradition of being respectful to elders. Soft or gentle handshakes were appropriate, especially from man to woman.

I remember discussing a criminal client of mine; she had a bit of an unusual first name and a two-word last name (adjective and noun). Your dad said wistfully: what a beautiful name. Because of that, I have never forgotten her name and find myself noting the beautiful names people have.

Unwavering integrity is an excellent descriptor for Sylvan. His work ethic was unmatched, and his writing style was clear and concise. I recall he had lovely handwriting. I don't know why that stuck with me.

I remember how devoted he was to your mother.

I know not all of this is appropriate for your purposes, but I have appreciated being able to walk down memory lane.

Jane Wipf Pfeifle
Seventh Judicial Circuit Court Judge

"TIL DEATH DO US PART"
SYLVAN AND MARGARET HAUFF
DECEMBER 23, 1955 – JUNE 29, 2020

Mr. and Mrs. Sylvan Hauff. St. Katherine's Episcopal Church, Martin, South Dakota. December 23, 1955.

Margaret and Sylvan Hauff, 1956. Photo taken in the Black Hills by the talented young photographer April Hauff.

Tracy, Age 2 Standing by a flower "pot" outside our first home in Winner, South Dakota.

The early 1960s
Sylvan and Margaret enjoy a rare night out with the neighbors. Probably New Year's Eve.

1983 Keystone, South Dakota, Professor Samuel's Old Time Photos.

1990s

2004

2008

Holding hands was a daily occurrence in their marriage.

2017

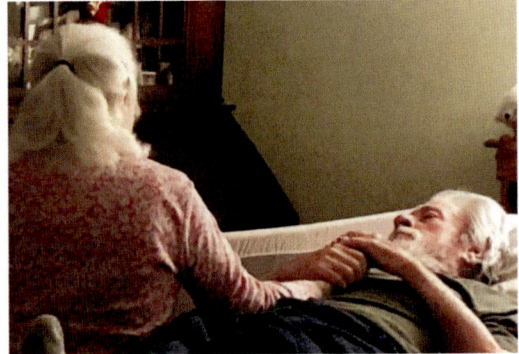

2018

2018

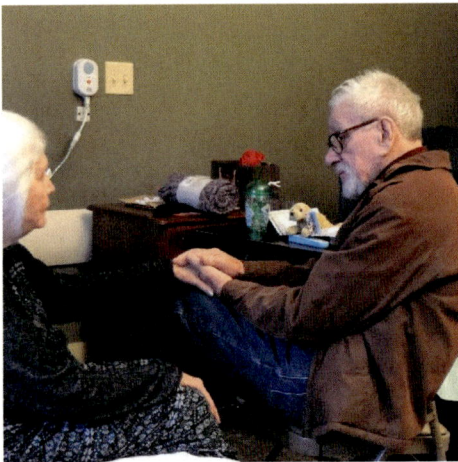

2019

2019

Sylvan and Margaret had seven children. April Gustafson, Steven Hauff, Tracy Hauff, Echo Rust, Alison Strauss, Brad Hauff, and Brian Hauff.

Seated left to right: Brad, Ruth (Brad's wife), Brian, April, Amy (April's daughter), Tracy, Echo, Alison, John Strauss (Alison's husband). Back row: Danny (April's son), Mike Gustafson (April's husband), Steven, Margaret, and Sylvan. 1999.

Sylvan was diagnosed with Alzheimer's in January 2014, and Margaret was diagnosed with Frontotemporal Dementia with Aphasia in May 2014. They remained in their own home with 24/7 assistance from family members and caregivers until January 2019, when they were moved to a long-term memory care facility. They were never separated, and even with his advancing Alzheimer's, Sylvan never forgot who Margaret was. I lived in their home to care for them from 2014 through 2015 and 2018 to 2019. I could hear Daddy tell Mama each night as they lay in bed, "I'm glad I got you, Maggie." To which she would reply, "Me, too." They talked to one another every night as they lay in bed, always holding hands, always kind and loving to one another. They knew the secret to a lifelong, affectionate marriage. Margaret was rapidly losing her speech and language skills—a horrible symptom of Frontotemporal Dementia—but Sylvan could understand what she was saying. At times, it was astonishing.

As his disease progressed, Sylvan's memory reverted back to his lonesome childhood. Every morning, I would make his breakfast, and we would sit at the kitchen table and talk. He would begin the conversation by asking me this question:

"Did you ever have to go to boarding school?"

"No, Daddy, I didn't."

"How come you never had to go?"

"Because you and Mama said you would never send your kids to boarding school."

He would nod, becoming silent while his eyes took on a faraway look before saying, "Boy, you're lucky."

"Yes, I am. We're all very lucky to have you and Mama as our parents."

This conversation, the nod of his head, never varied. He repeated it day after day after day. Sometimes more than once a day, but always at the kitchen table during a meal.

He would talk about classmates who ran away in the winter and froze to death trying to get home to their families. A happier memory was walking into Whiteclay, Nebraska, across the state line with his friends after they had combined all their change to buy a tin of chewing tobacco. He remembered sitting on the back stoop of the kitchen building with Mama while they shucked corn together. They would volunteer for this chore because it allowed them the rare opportunity to talk to one another.

It was hard for me to listen to his boarding school reminiscing, knowing that this particular subject was all he could think about now in his impaired mental condition. He discussed these memories matter-of-factly, never getting angry or upset when he talked about them. I would hug him and reassure him that those days were long gone and he had experienced a wonderful life since then. This would surprise him as he did not recall his admirable career with the federal government.

He began to speak Lakota more frequently. This also started at the kitchen table. He would ask for wakalyapi (coffee), aguyapi (bread), asanpi (milk), asanpi wigli (butter), talo (meat), and blo (potatoes.) He liked to tease his nurse, who visited him every week, by addressing her in Lakota. "Taku eciyapi he?" (What are you named?) She soon caught on and was able to respond with her name, which always made him chuckle. What caught my attention about Sylvan's phrasing in asking her name is that the Lakota 'he' used at the end of a sentence is a gender interrogative used by women asking a question. The correct way for a male to ask someone their name would have been "taku eciyapi hwo." Hwo signifies the male ending for a question. Albert White Hat, a Lakota language instructor, wrote, "When Lakota language was denied to the people, men started using the women endings. Male speakers who use "he" are either boarding-school products or were raised by women." Both of these were true in Sylvan's understanding of the Lakota language—he was raised in boarding school, and it would have been his mother who taught him the language at home.

Sylvan died June 29, 2020, while living in the memory care unit at the long-term care facility in Rapid City, South Dakota. I would love to write that he died peacefully, surrounded by all his loved ones, but that is not how it happened. The COVID-19 pandemic began in January 2020, and the United States was in full-blown panic over the global health emergency. The facility where my parents lived was practicing strict COVID lockdown regulations prohibiting visitation, and family members had not been able to see their loved ones since March 2020. Every nursing facility nationwide was unusually short-staffed; caregivers quit out of fear of contracting the virus, were already sickened with the virus, or were dealing with family members who were ill or dying.

I was contacted at 11 pm on the night of June 26th and told that my dad had been non-responsive for 24 hours and that I could see him in the morning. I went in as soon as possible; his eyes were closed and never re-opened. Unaware of his surroundings, he was visibly in pain. He had a black eye and a lump on his forehead. The nurse told me he had fallen, and the morning staff found him lying on the floor by his bed. That was the only explanation I could get out of anyone, no matter whom I talked to or how many ways I rephrased the question, "How did this happen?" For three days, hospice services never came to ease his discomfort— although I called them daily—and his children were only allowed to see him one at a time for one hour under stringent guidelines. The three days before he passed were terribly traumatic for my siblings and me. I have never experienced such agonizing grief and never imagined that this would be how our beloved father would leave this world. The illogical, unsympathetic healthcare guidelines imposed at that time by the Centers for Disease Control and Prevention (CDC) did not allow him to transition with the dignity and grace he deserved.

After Dad passed from non-Covid-related complications, I spent three months trying to get into the locked-down facility to see my mother. When I was finally allowed inside, I could feel my heart break when I saw the condition she was in, and I immediately began trying to get her out of that facility. Her poor state of health and inability to walk or communicate were due to neglect and malnutrition, not from her dementia. She had been walking fine before the lockdown but was now so weak it wasn't possible for her to carry her own weight, which had plummeted to 118 pounds. I would have taken her home with me, but my home was not handicapped accessible, inside or out; in fact, you couldn't even gain entrance to the main level without walking up two flights of stairs. Finding another place for her was difficult; all the nursing homes were full or unwilling to take on new residents. I was finally successful in January 2021, six months later. By this time, she was very ill, and I admitted her to the hospital, where she was diagnosed with severe dehydration and malnutrition, sepsis, a UTI infection, an eye infection, deep lesions and missing toenails on her feet, and an open weeping pressure ulcer on her sacrum the size of an orange. She had lost 40 pounds in three months. After being discharged from the hospital, she was in rehabilitation for two months. She was never able to walk again.

I tell you these unembellished facts not to shock or sadden you but because this recent period in the United States has become a controversial, unsettling part of our history, and this is only one family's story about the trauma created by the Coronavirus pandemic. COVID-19 caused suffering for millions of families worldwide from the deadly virus itself and the psychological strain caused by paranoia, confusion, and isolation. Families were involuntarily estranged from one another for over a year as social distancing and travel restrictions were implemented to slow down the spread of the contagious virus. Friends and family members voluntarily ended relationships over differences of opinion regarding mandated vaccinations and masking. Doctors, nurses, and hospital staff were exhausted, pushing themselves far beyond the expected standards for quality healthcare, and many experienced severe sleep deprivation. Some gave up and walked away from their jobs. The death rate for residents in nursing homes escalated to an all-time high, and the deaths were not always from the virus; thousands died from neglect.

The CDC made dreadful decisions regarding the lockdown of hospitals and nursing homes. Family members are essential when a loved one is in a long-term care facility, especially when they are in a memory care unit. These residents are the most vulnerable population, unable to care for themselves in any way, ranging from basic personal hygiene to essential survival needs such as hydration and food intake. Isolating the residents contributed to their physical, intellectual, and emotional decline. If there was ever a time when the health care providers needed family support, it was during the pandemic.

We had a proper burial for Sylvan on September 18, 2020. He was interred with military honors, a gun salute, and Taps at the Black Hills National Cemetery outside Sturgis, South Dakota. Attendance was limited to twenty immediate family members due to COVID-19 restrictions.

Margaret joined her husband in the afterlife on November 20, 2022. She was well cared for until the end, and four of her children were with her when she passed peacefully under hospice care. Her ashes were placed in Sylvan's grave on June 5, 2023.

A childhood bond shaped by loneliness and shyness forged an unbreakable union, and their love endured despite the trials of old age and cruel cognitive deterioration. Only death, with its final exhale, could part them.

BIBLIOGRAPHY

Books and Publications

Adams, David. The David Adams Journal. 1841. Edited by Charles E. Hanson, Jr. Missouri Historical Society.

Bettelyoun, Susan Bordeaux and Waggoner, Josephine. With My Own Eyes: A Lakota Woman Tells Her People's History. Edited by Emily Levine. University of Nebraska Press. 1998.

Bray, Kingsley. Crazy Horse, A Lakota Life. University of Oklahoma Press: Norman. 2008.

Brinks, Rose L. History of the Bingham Hill Cemetery, LaPorte & Bellvue, Colorado. Rose L. Brinks. 2005.

Chittenden, Hiram Martin. The American Fur Trade of the Far West. Lincoln: University of Nebraska. 1935

Clow, Richmond L. The Whetstone Indian Agency 1868-1872. South Dakota State Historical Society, 1977.

Dyck, Paul. The Sioux People of the Rosebud. Northland Press. 1971.

Hyde, George. Red Cloud's Folk, A History of the Oglala Sioux Indians. University of Oklahoma Press. 1937.

Livermont-Rooks Family Reunion Book. August 20, 1989. Rapid City, SD.

Means, Jeffrey. From Buffalo to Beeves: The Transformation of the Oglala Lakota Economy 1868-1889, University of Oklahoma. 2007.

McGuire, Jack and Shirley. Hauf/Germany. 2000.

Miller, Irma. French-Indian Families in America's West: Lessert (aka Claymore), Roy, Chatillon, Delor, Royer. Trafford Publishing. 1988.

Museum of the Fur Trade Quarterly. The best of goods for the least amount of money. Volume 44, Number 2. Summer 2008.

BIBLIOGRAPHY

Books and Publications

Nigl, Alfred, and Charles. Silent Wings, Savage Death: Saga of the 82nd Airborne's Glider Artillery in WWII. Graphic Publishers. 2007.

Nordyke, Phil. All American, All the Way: The Combat History of the 82nd Airborne Division in World War II, Voyageur Press. 2005.

Nordyke, Phil. Put Us Down in Hell: The Combat History of the 508th Parachute Infantry Regiment in World War II. Historic Ventures. 2012.

Parezo, Nancy J., and Angelina R. Jones. "What's in a Name? The 1940s-1950s 'Squaw Dress." American Indian Quarterly 33, no. 3. 2009.

Parkman, Francis. The Oregon Trail. University of Nebraska Press. Bison Books Edition. 1994.

Paul, R. Eli. Autobiography of Red Cloud, War Leader of the Oglalas. Montana Historical Society Press. 1997.

Powers, Marla N. Oglala Women: Myth, Ritual, and Reality. (Women in Culture and Society.) University of Chicago Press. 1988.

Robertson, Paul. The Power of the Land: Identity, Ethnicity, and Class Among the Oglala Lakota. Routledge. 2002.

Smiley, Jerome C. History of Denver. The Times-Sun Publishing Company. 1901. Chapters: XIX, XX, XXI, XXII, XXIII, XV.

U.S. Army Center of Military History. Ardennes-Alsace, The U.S. Army Campaigns of World War II. Government Documents. 1992.

White Hat, Albert Sr. Reading and Writing The Lakota Language. University of Utah Press. 1999.

WEBSITES

https://american-tribes.com/lakota

https://ancestry.com

https://archives.colorado.gov

https://carlisleindian.dickinson.edu

https://digital.denverlibrary.org

https://findagrave.com

https://guides.lib.uchicago.edu

https://historycolorado.org

https://history.fcgov.org

https://history.denverlibrary.org

https://lib.montana.edu

https://rememberingthechildren.org

https://sddigitalarchives.contentdm.oclc.org

https://ww2-airborne.us/units/508

https://wyohistory.org

INDEX

Made in the USA
Monee, IL
31 January 2025

11356439R00131